With his new book *Other*, English author Kester Brewin joins Peter Rollins from Ireland and David Dark from the US as leading public theologians for a new generation of thoughtful Christians. He moves gracefully from Scripture to philosophy to pop culture to sociology and back to Scripture again, offering fresh, honest, and needed insights at each turn. I look forward to keeping up with this important voice in the years ahead.

Brian D. McLaren

In our socially networked and technologically advanced world we remain surrounded by mystery: the mystery of others, the divine mystery and mystery that we are unto ourselves. *Other* masterfully explores how we might embrace this often complex reality and draws out how love of that which is other is central to the Christian experience. This is a work of rare beauty.

Peter Rollins

Love God, and love your neighbour as yourself: the golden rule is easy to say, but much harder to put into practice. Drawing on a mixture of sources from philosophy, history of science, sociology and theology as well as lots of personal anecdotes, Kester Brewin explores the challenge of understanding the self, as well as God and other people, as being the challenge to accept and love the 'other' – not just in theory, but in the ever-changing culture of the 21st century.

Maggi Dawn

Half-mystic and half hard-core intellectual, Brewin here offers us an intimate, personable, completely accessible and, at times, hauntingly beautiful engagement with the hard questions of emergence theology. This is a brilliant work. It illumines with reverence and care the paradox that is faith, even as it speaks, always with vigour, of love and the reality that lies at the centre of our not-knowing.

Phyllis Tickle

A book for mystics and poets and troubadours of a new world. Brewin invites you to look into the eyes of others and squint a little – to see the image of God. He dares you to see the world with new eyes – to look into the mirror and see one who is beloved, to look into the eyes of the orphan and see Christ, to look into the eyes of those whom we find hard to like and catch a glimpse of the One we love.

Shane Claiborne

Other

Kester Brewin

Embracing Difference in a Fractured World

HODDER

Unless indicated otherwise, Scripture quotations are taken from the Holy Bible,
New International Version. Copyright © 1979, 1984 by Biblica.
Used by permission. All rights reserved.
Other Scripture quotations are taken from *The Message*. Copyright © 1993, 1994,
1995, 1996, 2000, 2001, 2002. Used by permission of NavPress Publishing Group.

First published in Great Britain in 2010 by Hodder & Stoughton
An Hachette UK company
This paperback edition first published in 2011.

1

A CIP catalogue record for this title is available from the British Library

ISBN 978 1 444 70110 4

Typeset in Sabon by Hewer Text UK Ltd, Edinburgh
Printed and bound by Clays Ltd, St Ives plc

Hodder & Stoughton policy is to use papers that are natural, renewable and recyclable
products and made from wood grown in sustainable forests. The logging and manufacturing
processes are expected to conform to the environmental regulations of the country of origin.

Hodder & Stoughton Ltd
338 Euston Road
London NW1 3BH

www.hodderfaith.com

Acknowledgements

It's a well-worn cliché that 'Jesus didn't write a book, he formed a community.' I suppose I have had a little experience of both, and can confirm that work on the former is rather trying for the 'others' involved in the latter. So it falls to me to offer profound thanks to everyone around me – family and friends – for giving me time to scratch away when ideas come; this book, as a product of that time, is offered to all of you, and to Elias and Iris, my two patient children, in particular.

Finally, I must also thank Katherine Venn for not only being prepared to take the book on, but for her wise comments which helped knock the manuscript into shape, and all those who have contributed to discussions, online and off, who have enriched and fertilised the words that follow.

[PLMD]

Didn't the same God who made me, make them?

Job 31:15, *The Message*

Contents

Introduction: The dividing wall

'Of all the commandments, which is the most important?'

We are increasingly living in the society of the précis. Too busy to spend time reading in any great depth we scan excerpts from online searches, glance at executive summaries and instinctively flip to the back covers of books or skim through their pages looking for the key points. We tell ourselves this is all so modern of us, but perhaps it has always been the case. In chapter 12 of Mark's Gospel we find Jesus arguing with some religious leaders. They are debating taxation and marriage – money and sex, as ever – when another teacher overhears them and cuts straight to the chase: 'Of all the commandments, which is the most important?' The very picture of the modern man, he wants the condensed version. Forget the endless inventory of laws and sub-clauses; what's the two-line summary?

Perhaps you are skimming the first few paragraphs of this book, looking for that quick outline of what these pages are aiming to achieve. It would be churlish of me to deny you, and it is simply this: when asked by that teacher to summarise the entirety of God's message to God's people, what did Jesus mean by his reply?

'The most important [commandment] is this: Hear, O Israel, the Lord our God, the Lord is one. Love the Lord your God with all your heart and with all your mind and with all your strength. The second is this: love your neighbour as yourself' (Mark 12:29–31).

On the surface his answer seems so simple, the well-worn words comfortable to our hearing like an old pair of plimsolls. Perhaps the teacher went away satisfied – Jesus told him that he was 'not far from the kingdom' – but even a little digging reveals some complexity. Jesus' words are drawn from two different verses in the Torah, the Jewish scriptures. He had been asked for the *single* greatest commandment, but, refusing to respond in the singular, neither answer he gave came from the original ten given by God to Moses. This litany of 'thou-shalt-nots', set out at the beginning of Deuteronomy chapter 5, is passed over completely by Jesus. Instead, his quote about 'loving God with all we've got' is from the next section in chapter 6.

Jesus' choice for second greatest commandment is drawn from the other great Old Testament book of laws, Leviticus. Half way through chapter 19 we hear a tumble of prohibitions: do not steal, do not lie, do not deceive, do not swear, do not defraud your neighbour, do not pervert justice, do not slander, do not hate . . . But, again, it is from among these negatives that Jesus hauls out virtually the only statement phrased in the positive: *love your neighbour as yourself.*

How strange, how beautiful, that when asked for a quick summary of the entire Jewish law, Jesus opted to ignore the scores of forbidding words for two quotes about love. And so here is another précis, a few words to summarise the spirit that has driven this book: how can we better foster a faith that doesn't jump to harsh words of law, but longs instead to emphasise a love that moves in three directions – to God, to our neighbours and to ourselves?

x X x

Bethlehem, Palestine

I am beginning to write this book in Bethlehem, Palestine. It seems an appropriate place to start. I am travelling with a group of Christians from the UK. We are based at the InterContinental, on the north side of town, and sure enough people from many continents, Chinese, African, European, Russian, American, gather each mealtime for hummus, falafel, steak, rice, fruit, pastries and curries. The food, like the guest list, is a mishmash of flavours, all presented at one table; an opportunity to create experimental platefuls and culinary clashes.

Just down the road, in Manger Square, is the Church of the Nativity, the supposed site of the birth of the one we worship for breaking down the wall of hostility (see Eph. 2:14) between ourselves and others, between ourselves and God.[1]

The way in to the church is through a tiny stone opening, not more than four feet high. This main entrance was probably cut down to this size in the eleventh century by the Crusaders, who didn't want attacking Turkish soldiers to be able to ride their horses into the building. Justinian, emperor in the Byzantine period, had rebuilt the church in its current state on top of the original structure of AD 333. That had been built under the instruction of Helena, Constantine's mother, an early Christian who, before her emperor son took Christianity under his military wing, came to the Holy Land to build places of worship at well-attested sites from the Gospel stories. She knew this was the place of the nativity as, in an attempt to subdue the first Christians, the Romans had built a shrine to their own gods here.

Now the official religion of the Empire, Christianity had not been universally popular with the local people, and the church in Bethlehem was destroyed in the Samaritan Revolt of 529. Strangely though, the building was spared in 614 during the Persian invasion. According to legend, their commander, Shahrbaraz, saw frescos of the magi in the church, and, because of their Persian dress, ordered the church to be saved. The Crusaders later came to 'redeem' the church from the Muslims, and made their own expansions and adjustments, including the tiny doorway, through which no soldier could ride.

The inside of the church is dark, and very bare. Openings in the floor show mosaics discovered after the British Army repaired the building in 1922. The lead had been taken from the roof to make bullets for the First World War, and the structure and insides had suffered rain damage.

The main shrine is accessed down steep steps, down into a natural cave below the church. Contrary to the popular story, Mary and Joseph, our local guide explains, would not have stayed in an inn. Being only half a day's walk from Jerusalem, and with nothing but desert further south, there would be have been no market for one. Besides, they were coming to be recorded in a census at Joseph's ancestral town – they would have stayed with family. Or, at least, stayed in the cave below some family member's house, the place where the animals were kept safe at night. She was pregnant; they weren't yet married. It was a family embarrassment. They would be sheltered, but not welcomed inside.

The walls of the church are almost totally unadorned. There are a few still-visible frescos, mostly in bad condition, and we can still see the bullet marks left by the snipers who shot at those who took refuge in the church during the siege of 2002, which was sparked when Palestinian children threw rocks at Israeli soldiers, who returned fire with bullets. Enraged fathers then seized weapons and shot back, and the Israelis called in tanks and helicopters to hunt them down. They took refuge in the church with a number of families who had feared for their own safety amidst the exchanges of fire. Surrounded, the church became a fortress. The buildings around the church were commandeered or destroyed.

Just as in Jesus' day, every stone in this land seems melancholic with similar stories of a great history and a tragic present. He was questioned about the law in Jerusalem, in the temple courts, which even then would have hung heavy with the memories of exile and destruction. Now, only fifteen minutes drive away, our hotel sits just metres away from the thirty-foot concrete wall that encircles Bethlehem and the West Bank. With their Persian papers, the Wise Men would probably have been turned away. Each day from 3 a.m., we watch Palestinians begin to line up at the wall to wait to have their permits checked and checked again, their shoes removed and bodies searched so they can get to work for their Israeli employers by 8:30. The Israelis like having Palestinian labour. They are used to the heat, work hard, and can be paid less than the Israeli minimum wage. During the latest *intifada*, when the West Bank was locked down tightly, they experimented with cheap labour from Romania and other parts of Eastern Europe, but these workers drank on the job, and, with large influxes of itinerant working men, crime went up.

The Palestinian men, to avoid the Kafkaesque rigmarole of getting permits to work in Israel, used to just jump over walls and run across fields. Their employers encouraged it. They needed their workforce to be on time and regular. Now, with the concrete wall that snakes across the land like a vicious gash, this is almost impossible. The wall is there for security. Millions of tonnes of concrete poured and bulldozed, slicing roads and villages in two, an impermeable barrier between the two communities that will now not see or hear or touch one another again.

Love God, and love your neighbours, Jesus said, but all around the places where he walked are dividing walls and hostility. The Western Wall, the only remaining part of the Herodian Temple, stands below the Dome of the Rock mosque, just a stone's throw from the Church of the Holy Sepulchre – where the Christian sects argue so much over their shrine that a Muslim has to keep the keys to the building.

The watchtowers and tri-lingual road signage, the church bells and calls to prayer, the olives and salt-beef, the black-coated orthodox, the mobiles, cigarettes and cars; the Palestinian labourers caught between taking any work available so they can feed their families and the only work being the construction of the very walls and illegal settlements that ruin their lives; the mosaic of Israeli society, with Jews from Russia and Europe and the USA and Armenia, all with their pounding Arabs who have said that only by the space between them.

place, these few square miles where Jesus walked, and Abraham prayed and Mohammed dreamt, surely shows more clearly the problem of loving our gods and our neighbours and ourselves than any other place on earth.

Last night, after a bewildering day listening to Jewish settlers and Palestinian refugees and Israeli human-rights campaigners, having heard how God had given one people the land, while another people had lived and worshipped there since time immemorial, I returned to my hotel room to find a drunken businessman in the room next door, his television turned up very loud, singing his heart out to a song I couldn't understand, in a tonal system I didn't appreciate. I couldn't sleep, and was still angry about a silly incident with another member of the group earlier in the day where I'd felt misunderstood. I reached for the telephone – someone from reception should go and tell the singer to stop – but stopped myself. If *they* came up and told him to shut up, it would be clear *I* had complained. I knew I had to go and tell him myself. But I was afraid. He might misunderstand.

I had never met the man in the hotel room next to me before, and now I was going to have to. His loud singing and loud television were not intrinsically wrong; the problem was my proximity to them. His music had become my noise, and we were going to have to negotiate. I had faced a similar problem on the flight out to Tel Aviv. The lady in the seat in front of me had immediately reclined her chair fully and, not being the most svelte of women, I had ended up with the back of her seat pretty much on my knees. I was frustrated. I couldn't move. I felt claustrophobic. Her need to recline and sleep was a valid one but because neither of us could afford to pay for more space in Business Class – 'more space' being a handy euphemism for 'further away from other people who might get up my nose' – her need to sleep impinged on my need to move my legs.

Back at home a boy of sixteen or so had got a scooter, and would regularly race it up and down the road – and on the pavement – often with hands up and down the road the speed limit. The noise was annoying, and the little regard for to my children built an anger in me. They were clearly against the law and I wanted the law to punish them and protect me – but feared that if I confronted him I might become another victim of violence myself. The papers had recently carried a story of a young father like me, who'd challenged some boys like them and been left staggering to his death, clutching his bleeding chest.

The anger that rises in us in these situations – noisy neighbours, thoughtless fellow passengers – is not just about the physical discomfort we might experience. It is also about the powerlessness we feel. We want to be able to do something, and, if we knew the person, we'd have no problem doing so. But because they are 'other' we feel frightened, unable to predict how they might react, and annoyed that the people in charge aren't acting on our behalf.

Who is going to act on my behalf? Why aren't people thinking about my needs? Why am I being ignored? Why aren't the police making my street safer? Why isn't the government doing something? Why isn't justice being done? Why has God forsaken me?

It is easy to love those we love, but this is where Jesus' summary of the law is so subversive in its simplicity: the implication of his words and the context surrounding them is that we cannot rely on the legal system, on lists of 'do this' and 'don't do this', to enable us to feel comfortable living among others. In his reduction of the whole law to these three loves, what appears so simple a commandment turns out to be a radical and subversive manifesto for living in a complex world, a key to unlocking all that is at the centre of our conflicts – internal, communal, theological and political.

From the personal to the local, through the communal, municipal, national, global and into the divine universal, the problem of loving 'the other' is, I believe, absolutely fundamental to the problems we face at all zoom-levels of our lives. Our internal fights with depression and doubt, our concerns for our neighbourhoods and ancient lands and our young people who carry knives and spit curses, our immigration laws, our over-zealous child protection laws that stop us taking our neighbour's kids to football practice, our dealings with asylum-seekers, our anger that our faith is being diluted or poisoned by gays and women, our fears that fundamentalists are going to take power, or, with a home-ma device made from a recipe concocted in a training camp on the other side of the world, take our lives . . . running through all of these concerns is a common fear – that of 'the other'. Running parallel to that fear is our fear that, in among all this, we are not being listened to, our rights are not being respected; we are, in short, not being loved.

Jesus summarised the whole of Jewish law with these twin commands to love God and love our neighbours as we love ourselves. He could have gone further and given the teacher just three words: *love the other*. The opposite of this – self-love – is narcissism. It is easy to love the parts of ourselves that are popular, the parts of our bodies that are beautiful, the parts of lives of which we are proud. It is easy to love the God who answers our prayers, easy to love the God who comforts us and saves us from distress. It is easy to love those neighbours we have who are generous, those neighbours who are polite and don't disturb us.

It is easy to love what is *lovely*; but we are called to love what is *other*. This is why Jesus' summary of the law holds such contemporary importance for us: our faith, our communal lives and our selves have all become much more narcissistic. The reasons for this are many, but I want to highlight the fact that just 100 years or so ago our village would have been our world. Now, the world is our village. Our everyday exposure has been blown open from the small, homogenous local scale of static family, trade and relationships to the global, heterogeneous scale of virtual connection, fluid trading patterns and scattered family. An increased narcissism – a cocooning instinct that focuses on the self – has thus developed as a coping mechanism in a bewilderingly plural world.

In a world where I can believe what I like, I choose to believe in a protectionist, fundamentalist, exclusive God. In a world where I can be friends with whosoever I like, I choose to befriend those who are strikingly similar to me in outlook and income. And in a world where I can be whatever I want to be, I choose to construct a public façade made up only of those parts of myself that I feel others will love me for.

8

Is this not simply a case of improved self-confidence? We know what we like, whom we like and what we believe – aren't we simply sticking by these principles? Research does show that self-confidence is increasing in Western societies, but so too is anxiety and depression. This apparent contradiction appears to be resolved by the realisation that,

> Increasing anxieties about how we are seen and what others think of us [have], in turn, produced a kind of defensive attempt to shore up our confidence in the face of those insecurities. The defence involves a kind of self-promoting, insecure egotism which is easily mistaken for high self-esteem. . . . The recognition that what we have seen is the rise of an insecure narcissism – particularly among young people – rather than a rise in genuine self-esteem now seems widely accepted.[2]

It is easy to love what it *lovely*; but we are called to love what is *other*. Who then is this 'other'?

It is the other within myself, the parts of me that I hide in the dark, the half-fictional parts I parade and boast. What would it mean to truly love this self of mine?

It is the other within God, the divinity I cannot fully know or understand who does not answer my prayers and does not provide comfort; the incarnate and yet ever-hidden who infects my dreams and won't let me let go. What would it mean to love this God with all of my self?

And it is the other within the world I inhabit, the neighbours who are noisy, the street-people who are smelly, the immigrants who are strange.

In Luke's version of the story of Jesus' summary of the law, the teacher asks him the obvious follow-up question, 'who is my neighbour?' Jesus replies with the story of the Good Samaritan. A man, lying dying in the road having been brutally beaten and robbed, is ignored by two righteous but fearful priests, but then helped by a passing Samaritan. At different points of history he might have told the story in terms of Protestants and Catholics, or Sunnis and Shias, or Americans and Communists, or Evangelicals and gays – the point remains the same. The person who acted with grace and mercy towards 'the other' was the one who was the true neighbour.

This is another strange answer from Jesus. He had been asked who his neighbour was; the reply he gave was to explain how to be a good neighbour, the implication being that there is no one who is not our neighbour, no one to whom we should not show mercy. The 'other' in the world around me is *everyone* around me.

x X x

London, England

I have struggled with this personally. I live in a relatively comfortable neighbourhood in London. A young boy was shot dead in a street less than a mile away yesterday, but, despite our physical proximity, I have little contact with the networks that he was a part of. Compared to the huge properties behind secure walls that some live in, or the gentle villages in the far-off countryside, I am on the front line of urban criminality. Compared to millions of others in cities like my own, and those in developing nations, I am one of the very, very lucky tiny percentage of wealthy people in the West with a solid home to live in and fairly peaceful streets within which to walk.

So who is my neighbour? To whom should I be offering grace, mercy and money?

In her excellent book *Making Room*, Christine Pohl has explored the tradition and practice of Christian hospitality through the ages and concluded that it is one that is currently in crisis. Far from being something at the heart of what we are about as Christians, as it was for so long in the early church, hospitality is now seen as 'a nice extra if we have the time or the resources'.[3] Ironically, it is partly due to the pioneering work in care for the sick and poor that the Church began – and ended up handing over to the state – that we now perceive so little need to be hospitable in the ancient sense. We are well-resourced people, and rarely have the experience of being a vulnerable stranger. We pay our taxes and expect social services to deal with the poor and sick and homeless. We think of ourselves as hospitable hosts: we give a good dinner party and welcome people when they come to our home.

But, as Pohl explains, the ancient practice of hospitality has always been about welcoming the other, the stranger. It has always been about stopping in the road to tend to the suffering and broken, rather than hurrying past to be on time to bless those at a religious meeting.[4] As to who these 'strangers' might be today, she identifies them as 'those who are disconnected from basic relationships that give persons a secure place in the world', and continues, 'the most vulnerable strangers are detached from family, community, church, work and polity'.[5]

This is what I have struggled with. Should I be actively seeking to open my doors to welcome in the homeless, the addicted and the convicted? Despite having two young children, the answer must remain yes – I must be prepared to do this. Of course, as Christians we are meant to function corporately – as a body – rather than just as individuals, yet while I believe it is certainly true that our faith communities must make themselves places of such radical hospitality, this cannot then abdicate me of responsibility for more local acts in my own home.

I have only had rare experience of this. On the evening of Christmas day last year, my family were staying at my sister's house in another part of London. We had eaten well, the children were in bed and we were in the middle of sharing some liturgy and reflection when the doorbell went. A tramp was outside and had nowhere to go. It felt easy with us all there and no pressures on time or work: we welcomed him in, got his feet clean and filled him with sweet tea before getting him somewhere to sleep. I was even able to make good use of the pairs of socks I'd inevitably been given as presents earlier in the day.

This, however, was an uncommon experience and it troubles me that my own practice falls so far short of the simple instruction Jesus gave. Should I be doing more to help the needy of my city, my country – and those of other countries? Yes. Jesus' command to love our neighbours is a command to love all strangers precisely because we too have been strangers to God and welcomed in. The Jews were strangers in Egypt – they knew what it was like to be persecuted and vulnerable in a strange place – and it was precisely because they had suffered like this that they were urged to treat strangers *as if they were neighbours*.[6]

Yet, while I remain troubled by the rarity with which I am able to fulfil my responsibility to be hospitable to the stranger, I believe that part of our duty of hospitality is more subtle and local. Yes, I must do better to find ways to welcome the homeless, the refugees and the poor who are detached from family, community and work, but I also need to be aware that our modern world is leaving so many feeling a profound sense of detachment, despite having the outer trappings of home, job, family and even church. As Pohl puts it, 'Hospitality builds and reinforces relationships among family, friends, and acquaintances. It is one of the pleasures of ordinary life. Yet even this most basic form of hospitality is threatened by contemporary values, life-styles, and institutional arrangements which have helped to foster the sense that we are all strangers, even to those to whom we are related.'[7]

In a sense we are all in need of help from Samaria; and we are all blinded, bruised and battered by this road we are on. Our haughty and self-important religion appears disinterested, unsympathetic. We are not poor, but our lives are impoverished; we are not homeless, but we know no secure place to go; we may not be unemployed, but we know not how to overcome our apathy and fruitfully apply our energies. In our economic fullness and confident tourism we so rarely experience the need for true hospitality. But in this consumerist satiation we are removed from any interaction with the gift, and so, though our stomachs may be full and our roofs impermeable, we are also removed from the empathy and generosity that actually lies at the heart of hospitality. We are not hungry, but we still crave this feeling of being loved and cared for by others.

So part of our calling to love the other will be to make sure the hungry are fed and the homeless cared for – and let us be vigilant because, with financial turmoil affecting economies in all parts of the world at the time of writing, there are going to be so many more in this situation – but another part of it will be to remove our dollar-tinted spectacles in order that we might see the lonely, the spiritually homeless and hungry, the depressed, the hungry ghosts who float online in search for love and acceptance, and work out how to best love them too.

What does it mean to love myself? Who is my neighbour? What do I love, as Augustine said, when I love my God?

Jesus, the Word made Flesh, so often speaks words that refuse to bounce, words that drill down beneath our flesh to the core of our hopes and fears. Deceptive in their simplicity, he shows in these few short phrases that in order to be whole we must engage the other, but also appreciates that it is our need to feel loved and included that makes us fearful and conflicted when we have to perform that engagement. He knows that we are all Samaritans, all wounded people on the road, busy and (mostly) sincere believers trying to do our best to love our God.

From my hotel room's Internet connection in Bethlehem I read news of a bus driver back in London, who has made it clear to his employers, and the press, that he will not drive a vehicle carrying a cheeky advertisement promoting atheism. He didn't want to take a stand, but now feels he has to. What is less clear is whether he has in the past taken any stand on sexually provocative shower-cream adverts, or if he made remaining silent a condition of carriage for any atheist passengers, or if he has refused to drive his bus with advertising that tantalises the poor with offers of cheap loans or high interest debt consolidation services. We all, like him, have our blinkers, like the commentator on a national news website recently who called for 'religion to be banned in the

Middle East', not thinking who might enforce the banning, and that doing so would itself amount to an act of dogma.

We cannot have a world without ideologies, and these ideologies are always going to be plural and, to a greater or lesser extent, have places of disagreement. The answer is not to ditch God, but to live a life in love with love. For some of us, that will mean faithfulness to the 'big Other' we know as Love incarnate; for others it will be a pursuit of the higher ideals 'liberty, fraternity and equality'. Either way, Jesus' commands to love ourselves, love one another, and love God-who-is-Love, are inextricably bound together. And it is this assemblage of love that I want to explore in these pages: the only proper way to a fulfilled Self is through engagement with 'the other', and the only peaceful way to better love of God is through a shared pursuit of that God.[8]

Of course, this talk of love can seem easy on paper; words of love can be like spun sugar, creating an appearance of substance, but melting into nothing on touch. So we must be careful of too much speech. We must ensure that, rather than turning always to texts and statements that read us our rights and harden our beliefs that we *are* right, we put our books down and step out into the corridor and knock on our neighbour's door, or lean forward and tap them on the shoulder. It is when they answer that our words and thoughts about God must metamorphose into graceful action. A smile, not a glare. 'Excuse me, but would you mind . . .'

The man singing in the room next door, the woman in the aeroplane seat in front of me: in both cases they didn't mind. Embarrassed, the man in the next room turned the music down and was profusely apologetic. We shared no language other than gestures, but both left laughing. The lady in front of me on the aeroplane had been badly bitten on her leg, and was in genuine pain. She apologised and I moved seats for her. I never did call the police over the young guy across the road. Seeing him leaving his house one day I went over and spoke to him with as much levity as I could muster, one of the children in my arms as some sort of ammunition. He was genuinely sorry, and, while I wouldn't patronise him with the term 'friend', he is now someone I'll shout hello to. He's graduated from scooter to car and I popped over to tell him he'd left his lights on the other day. Doubtless he drives like a lunatic, but not on my street at least.

The bitterness does not always run away so easily. In Bethlehem, it seems it will take a very long time. When Mary and Joseph arrived there, they found little welcome. They were tolerated and sheltered, but only as animals were. The country was under occupation, the people oppressed by hard religion and harsh taxation. But through all of this, into their temporary home among cattle, with a new baby born in scandalous circumstances, they welcomed others. The miracle of the shepherds and wise men is not just that they came, but that they were invited in and treated as neighbours, not strangers. Poor farm hands, outcasts from polite Jewish society, and strange astrologers from other religions and cultures. This incarnation, this breaking through of the divine other into our midst, and the tiny breaking out of peace and acceptance that it brought, became possible when a young girl loved God enough to believe, and loved herself enough to accept that gift.

x X x

Here, there

In one of the choruses that he wrote for a 1937 play *The Rock* T. S. Eliot, in the voice of a 'Stranger', posed a series of rhetorical questions about our life in cities: do we live so close together because we love each other and want to make community, or because we want to make money from our neighbours?[9] His questions remain pertinent because our world is urbanising. We are forced to huddle ever closer together in cities, but I believe it is possible to see this movement as spiritually enriching, for it is only because of these huddles that the Stranger gets to ask their questions, and only in them that we get to explore what our cities mean.

What is becoming very clear is that our cities mean close exposure to radical difference. We encounter those from very different backgrounds, very different cultures and with very different value systems. Moreover, we encounter those with vastly different means to us. In *The Spirit Level*, Richard Wilkinson and Kate Pickett's seminal study into how we might improve the quality of life for *all* levels of society – less violence, greater feelings of wellbeing, better health outcomes – an extraordinarily powerful truth is uncovered: it is *income inequality* that is the single greatest impediment to quality of life.[10] In a city or nation with a greater difference between rich and poor there will always be more violence, more anxiety in all stages of life, poorer health and less general wellbeing, regardless of whether the general standard of living of that country is higher or lower. In our increasingly urbanised and consumer-driven world their thoroughly researched thesis gives us not only a policy principle within which our democratic institutions should work, but an ethic towards which we should all strive, and which is shown to result in better outcomes for all: social equality. A reduction, in other language, of the distance between ourselves and the other.

Reducing income inequality is going to be fundamentally important, but will not of itself increase our engagement with the other. It will lay the foundations for a more fruitful engagement, but this engagement will still need to happen.

How can we achieve this? The mechanics of change fascinate me, and having worked in and around many organisations I have come to believe that change should be emergent, rather than 'top down'. In many ways this book is an attempt to both widen and narrow the horizon of emergent change within corporations to that of the societal and the personal; to consider how we might begin to set in motion some of the mechanics of change towards this more equal and just world that Wilkinson and Pickett show so convincingly is the only way for all to improve their life outcomes.

T. S. Eliot continues to press us: what will our answer to the Stranger be? Are we only here to make money, or are we here to make community? If it is money, then the Stranger may still be welcomed, if only to be fleeced, and Wilkinson and Pickett assure us that violence will increase and wellbeing fall. But if it is community, then, the Nativity story tells us, we must welcome the Stranger as an equal, as one we need in order to make our meanings more complete. As shepherds and astrologers, young girls and men, we must pursue this meaning, this God, together. Not that we might beat one another and 'win', but that we might learn to see the divine in one another, and even in ourselves, in the hope that one day, we might together encounter this other face to face as equals.

> It is easy to love what is lovely, but we are called to love what is other.
> It is easy to love what is familiar, but we are called to love what is strange.
> It is easy to love what is comforting, but we are called to love what is disturbing to us.

The aim of this book is therefore very simple. I want to examine what Jesus' summary of the law might mean by meditating on the three 'others' apparent in his words: the other within the self, the other within God and the other within our society. What might love for the other mean in these three different dimensions?

This simple question must then lead us to a recognition that love is complicated, interconnected, emergent and evolving. It is also a love that must be lived, and so I will end with some practical examples of how we might begin to live in ways that will lead us to equilibrium within ourselves, equality with others, and into the mystery of communion with a God who stooped down to Bethlehem to become our equal too.

PART ONE

LOVING THE OTHER WITHIN THE SELF

If God is so important, and our neighbour central to who we are and what we believe, why begin with loving the self? The question is an important one, as it can affect our attitudes to dealing with conflict at many different levels. Is it always right to spend time dealing with problems at home before even attempting to sort out problems abroad? Should the UK first deal with every last question of human rights before moving to critique the records of any other nation? Should I make sure all is at peace in my own home before trying to negotiate peace between the rival gangs fighting in the park?

The answer, typically, appears to be no, and yes. We cannot wait until everything is at peace before we try to make peace elsewhere, because if we did wait we would be waiting forever. But nor can we begin to try to make peace elsewhere if we are so compromised within our own self that attempting to do so would probably make matters worse. We must take the plank out of our own eye first before attempting extraction of the speck from our neighbour's eye. But perhaps embedded within this wisdom is a suggestion that we also cannot wait for total ocular purity – we remove planks before we turn to our neighbour's specks, but don't spend valuable resources on eyewash and goggles for ourselves while our neighbour continues to suffer.

'The hardest step in any revolution,' as the singer Michael Franti has put it, 'is the personal revolution.' We begin, therefore, with the self, but only *because* we have one eye on our neighbour's suffering, only because we are concerned with the wider change that we want to see.

In my previous book, *The Complex Christ*, I set out some ideas about how we might approach the problem of change. Changing things is difficult and time-consuming, and I set out some principles of emergent, bottom-up change, arguing that this would, over time, give rise to the most effective results. I still very much hold to this view, and yet felt stirred by a gentle rebuke in theologian Miroslav Volf's seminal book *Exclusion and Embrace*: 'Theologians should concentrate less on social arrangements and more on fostering the kind of social agents capable of envisioning and creating just, truthful and peaceful societies, and on shaping a cultural climate in which such agents will thrive.'[1]

If *The Complex Christ* was a meditation on 'social arrangements', then I can think of no better way of describing these pages than as a meditation on how to best foster good 'social agents'. As Volf later puts it, we need to find out 'what kind of selves we need to be in order to live in harmony with others'.[2]

Certainly, what Richard Wilkinson and Kate Pickett have set out in *The Spirit Level* is that harmony with others is only going to come when we become more equal with others. The hard numbers tell us that social wellbeing – the just, truthful and peaceful societies that Volf writes of – will only come when the difference between rich and poor is minimised. But how can we achieve greater equality with 'the other'? How can we foster 'visionary social agents' to bring about the huge changes that will be required?

One of the common criticisms of my last book was that it wasn't practical enough, that it simply didn't explain clearly *how* to create an emergent faith community. This is quite true, and was quite deliberate. It was uncomfortable to be left with some thinking to do. We don't like to have to think. We like to be *told* exactly what it is we should do. We want a programme to follow, a recipe to guarantee a good set of outcomes. And this was precisely what I was trying to avoid in that piece. Why? Because recipes only account for local taste. Far better to foster a love of cuisine, and encourage people to seek out indigenous ingredients. So, it's not that I think that practicalities don't matter, rather I believe that they matter too much, so much in fact that it is not for me, from afar, to explain to you what you should do and which particular social arrangements will work best.

The question about 'within what sort of cultural climate will good social agents naturally arise?' leads us to ask questions which I simply cannot answer. What is your local culture? What is your local climate? What affects these local conditions? What sort of conditions, in your home, in your street, your city and country, will allow equality to flourish and goodness to evolve and emerge naturally? I cannot address those specifics, only reflect on ways in which we might be able to shape our own cultural climates.

It is to this that I will turn in the last section, where I outline some practical examples of things going on in and around my city, but before I do that it is vital that we understand the vectors that will lead us there. We must resist the temptation to seek quick solutions, off-the-shelf programmes which we can buy into. As I have previously written, genuine change is a complex, emergent process which begins from the ground up, from the inside, and evolves in response to the interplay of local connections. It is out of these environments that wider cultural and political change will grow and, while I want to be ambitious and tackle how we might begin to face these huge issues, I need first to heed Volf's advice: *what kind of selves do we need to be in order to live in harmony with others?*'

The Slovenian philosopher Slavoj Žižek concurs with this approach. In the introduction to his book *Violence*, he recounts a joke that was told about Lenin, whose mantra 'learn, learn, learn' plastered every Russian school wall. The joke runs like this: Marx, Engels and Lenin were asked if they'd prefer a wife or a mistress. Marx, seen as more conservative, goes for the wife; Engels, more liberal, the mistress. But Lenin says he'll have both. Why? So he can tell his wife that he's with his mistress, and his mistress that he's with his wife, so that he can 'go to a solitary place to learn, learn, learn'.

This, Žižek counsels, 'is what we should do today when we find ourselves bombarded with mediatic images of violence. We need to learn, learn, learn what *causes* this violence.'[3] Before we protest about the terrible violence we see in our cities and across the world, we must, he goes on to expound, withdraw to some third place, away from wife and mistress, and reflect on the violence within each of us and the violence inherent in the systems we inhabit.

It seems this is then our first conclusion: time spent in self-reflection is a necessary precursor to sensitive and effective communion with the 'other', and the oscillation between the twin poles of withdrawal and communion must be maintained.

Allan Kaplan, founder of the Community Development Resource Association in Cape Town, South Africa, has long worked with NGOs and other development organisations of all sizes across Africa and Europe. Moving away from the colonial-tinged donor/receiver model of aid and development, he writes instead about 'social process', and urges those involved in development to reflect on the ways in which they are involved in the dynamic rhythm and form of these process flows: 'As social practitioners – whether consultant, leader or constructive participant – we are there to work with the organism's process. As such, we have to learn to read and recognise the underlying patterns, and help unblock or adjust, so that the ongoing process of development may unfold once more.'[4]

We will explore later how we might use this model of social practice as we begin to engage with the other, but what is pertinent to note now is that a vital precursor to this engagement with the processes of another organism or system is consciousness of our *own* flows and processes. As Kaplan notes, 'Individuals and social organisms, endowed with the gift of self consciousness, have the possibility of becoming aware of their own processes, and thus become responsible for their own evolution, rather than merely subjected to that evolution.'[5]

This is our simple goal in self-reflection: to become conscious of our 'selves' – to better understand the flows and processes that make up who we are, and through this consciousness, to evolve into more responsible organisms that can then go on to help others achieve the same thing.

If there is no reflection, then we will never work out what shadows within ourselves may be causing division. Similarly, if there is no expectation of movement beyond self-reflection, it is no more than navel-gazing; our heads may begin bowed in prayer, but if they stay there examining the remains of our umbilicals, we can only expect a stiff neck. In this vein Žižek is very critical of what he calls 'Western Buddhism' for this 'fetishisation' of meditation, and we must be aware of this danger as reflective Christians too. In *On Belief* he writes that

> the 'Western Buddhist' meditative stance is arguably the most efficient way for us to fully participate in the capitalist dynamic while retaining the appearance of mental sanity. [It] is a fetish – you are well aware how worthless this spectacle is – what really matters to you is the peace of the inner Self to which you know you can always withdraw.[6]

We must avoid this compromised stance by balancing contemplation and action, but must also be aware that balance is notoriously difficult to achieve. 'We tend to fall asleep within the lullaby comfort of a particular bias,' Kaplan notes, going on to reflect that 'it is comfortable precisely because it is relieved of the tension between opposites'.[7] I am sure we can each think of those who are peacefully drifting off in this 'lullaby comfort' of either permanent contemplation or frenetic action; we must recognise that it is only in the tension of these two poles that creative energy and genuine development will occur.

x X x

The reflective self: desert, bad faith, being

We begin with the self, we begin with the log in our own eye, we begin at home, but all the time we will be carrying the knowledge

25

with us that true reflection will never leave us unchanged, and thus will never leave our relationship to the world and the systems we are connected to unchanged either. Self consciousness, an appreciation of who we are and what flows and fields make up our life, will inevitably lead to our desire to see the flows of others unblocked and running free, whether this means lifting them out of poverty or releasing them into artistic practice.

It is instructive to read the Gospels this way: we see Jesus born and baptised, but then spending time in the desert before beginning his subsequent ministry. It is here that he begins to wrestle with exactly who he is and what he has been called to do. This time has become popularised as him facing temptation, but I believe that it is not simply about him learning to resist. His fasting, praying and, we assume, meditating, was a time to centre his self, to anchor himself in the right place before embarking on a ministry to others.

The symbolic forty days he is said to have spent here may seem like a long time, but would have been laughed at by later Christian ascetics who spent years and years living alone in caves in the desert. Aside from Žižek's critique of their asceticism as fetishistic, one wonders what Jesus' reaction to them would have been had he met one. Would the monk have chastised Jesus for being such a short-termer? Or would Jesus have encouraged the monk to move on from refining the self so harshly, and brought them back into community?

I believe he would. Jesus' time spent in the desert was essential, yes, but only in that it was essential *preparation*. In order to deal with the other, he first needed a secure sense of self, but he did not wait until *everything* was secured. Later passages in the Gospels show us that Jesus still had doubts and questions, and had to withdraw periodically to wrestle with them.

As we begin to think about 'what kind of selves we need to be in order to live in harmony with others', we would be wise to follow Jesus' pattern. Whether introvert or extravert, time spent alone to reflect on our own lives is vital, for without it we lose a sense of exactly who we are. In the incessant business of modern life – rushing to and from work, dropping kids off, catching trains and gasping to get to meetings – we often lack quality time to simply be, to solidify the boundaries of our selves and resist the city's attempts to count us as simply part of the crowd.

I cannot tell you who you are, or do that work of reflection for you. But, over the course of the next few pages, I want to hold up some reflective surfaces, some sketches of some of the sorts of selves our postmodern, technologically advanced world might be forming. They will be caricatures only, but, as with that form, may help us to see our selves more truly, selves that are under constant reformation by family, story, joy and pain. What elements of these selves will help us to live in harmony will only become apparent as we take the time to get to know them. It is in the mode of Jesus' desert experience that I want to argue we can best do that.

To use another metaphor, the philosopher Martin Heidegger wrote of becoming more aware of the 'clearing' (*Lichtung*) – the suddenly opening space in the midst of the packed woods, where light can more easily penetrate: 'In the midst of beings as a whole an open place occurs. There is a clearing, a lighting. Only this clearing grants and guarantees to us humans a passage to those beings that we ourselves are not, and access to the being that we ourselves are.'[8]

Jesus spent time in the desert and returned, yet in Heidegger's sense it is not that we come upon these 'clearings' at various times along our journey, rather that the clearing already exists within us, and we need to become better aware of it. In other words, it is not necessary for us to spend days fasting under the fierce light of the desert sun; rather, we must carry that desert place, that differently lit place, within us and learn to pause periodically to centre our vision on it. It is only here, as Heidegger points out, that we will begin to be able to engage both with others, and with the core of ourselves. It is in the light that our boundaries will find clarity.

As he sat in a Parisian café, drinking coffee and smoking in the sun, the Existentialist philosopher Jean-Paul Sartre described this need for a life lived *in lichtung* in different terms. A life outside of the clearing, he put it, would be a life lived in 'bad faith'.

The story goes that as he observed the bustle of the café around him, he noted that the waiter serving him was acting in a *far-too-waiterly way*. In other words, despite the radical freedom that Sartre ascribed to every human being, this waiter appeared to be restricted by an obligation to play the role of waiter as others expected it. He was thus reducing himself to something approaching an automaton, a robot programmed to do exactly what a waiter ought.

Looking further round the café, Sartre saw – in fact he must have imagined it – a girl out on a date. During the date, the man moves his hand and places it on hers. The girl, thinking about the situation in a disembodied way, decides that it is very possible that the man is only doing what he is doing because he is attracted to her physical beauty, and he is not much interested in her as a person. However, since he is just touching her hand, and her hand is not *really* an inner part of her self, she does not need to decide at this moment what she feels and whether she will have sex with him. She can do so later.

For Sartre, both the waiter and the girl are living in 'bad faith'. His reasoning for this view is based on the fact that humans are different from objects in that our consciousness is 'non self-identifying'. A table is a table because it fulfils all the properties that we attribute to tables. But even if we made an infinite list of all the properties of a person, we would never succeed in fully describing their personality. In other words, we aren't simply human because we do human-like things.

This is why Sartre is critical of the waiter: he is feeling an obligation to display the attributes of a waiter, even though there is nothing that should force him to do so. However, he is also equally critical of the girl because, even though she refuses to be described by the facts of her actions, her transcendent position

– positing her hand as something outside of her self – is also a denial of the true situation.

Sartre thus sets up this paradox: we are what we are, but precisely part of our being is that we are *not* simply what we are. In his language, we have both *facticity* and *transcendence*: there are undeniable facts about who we are and what properties or attributes we have as people, but while these things can be used to describe us, they can never fully do so. There is always something 'beyond' about us too.

Žižek puts this in more theological terms in his verbal duel with Radical Orthodox theologian John Milbank:

> I am here as part of substantial reality, and what I am I am at the expense of others, demanding my share of reality. But this is not what makes me a unique person . . . What distinguishes me are not my personal idiosyncrasies, the quirks of my particular nature, but the abyss of my personality.

> This is how man is made 'in the image and likeness of God': what makes a human being like God is not a superior or even divine quality of the human mind . . . It is only at the level of person, . . . this abyss beyond all properties, that man is 'in the image of God.'[9]

To live in 'good faith' then, to live a life in 'the clearing', is to accept something of the paradox of who we are. By accepting both our facticity and transcendence we are, to rework Heidegger's original meaning slightly, attempting to access this 'passage to those beings that we ourselves are not, and access to those that we are'. We are also thus attempting to live as we were designed to be, in the image of God.

It is perhaps to this paradox that Jesus turned his thoughts in his time in the desert. Indeed, it is perhaps this paradox that was towards the heart of all his moments of anguish that we read about in the Gospels. Was he God, or was he man? The facts were plain: he was physically alive and in time. He felt pain and emotion. He had a name, parents, family, friends, skills – all pointing to a strong human facticity. But there was something else too. Something that transcended these physical attributes, these lists of human properties. There was an abyss of divine person within him.

The miracle of the incarnation is that Jesus refused to collapse this paradox of his existence either way. He would not simply give in to human needs – turn stones into bread and eat – but nor would he disappear into unreachable transcendence, jumping unscathed from the temple. In the Passion we see the endgame of this battle with the devil to force Jesus into bad faith one way or the other. Here on the cross is a man in full physical pain. The nails are no pretence. The thorns are no metaphor. And yet, just at the moment where Jesus appears to have collapsed into facticity, his God abandoning him to death, we see him transcend that death by rising again. The hopelessness of Easter Saturday is that Jesus was nothing more than a man. But the joy of Easter should not be in the realisation that he was God, but that he was still *both divine and human*.

It is into this existential paradox that we cast ourselves when we follow the path of Jesus because, as Žižek has pointed out, Irenaeus' motto that 'God made Himself man, that man might become God', needs to be completed with the admission that 'God made Himself man, that man might become God *who made Himself man*'. [10] In other words, our desire to repair God's image in us is a task that makes us simultaneously both more God-like and more human.

Unfortunately we see far too many Christians living in 'bad faith'. One of the implications of Sartre's thoughts is that we need to be very careful before denominating ourselves as anything, whether that be 'Christian', 'British' or 'liberal'. For example, in calling myself 'Christian' I risk either over-emphasising the facticity of this denomination, by setting out a list of Christian attributes that I need to live/play up to, or over-emphasising the transcendent, by declaring that my status as Christian is simply a matter for God, unconnected to my actions. (In very broad brush-strokes, we might see the evangelical wing of the Church, with its emphasis on practical Bible teaching for right living, as over-emphasising the facticity of our faith, and the high/Catholic wing of the Church as overemphasising the transcendent nature of our faith.)

Jesus, though, refused to collapse this paradox either way. Indeed, what is interesting about Judeo-Christian history is that we are engaging a God who is well aware of this paradox. This is a God who *has a name, but will not and cannot be named*. Yahweh, which is meant neither to be said nor written, is both a name and not-a-name; to call yourself 'I am existence' is to put yourself above any requirement for denomination.

So as we again reflect on the sorts of selves we need to be to live peacefully with others, our reflection leads us into two connected paradoxes:

- The energy of our existence is in the tension between facticity and transcendence,
- The rhythm of our journey is found in the tension between action and contemplation.

It would be fruitless to sit and wonder until we had worked out a solution to this conundrum, just as it would be foolish to march out with no appreciation for it. The fire that enters us at Pentecost is the searing desert sun and the light falling through the thinning canopy: the Spirit is Heidegger's clearing, the wisdom of Jesus that understands that we are being and doing, adoration and action, and human and Other. It is only as we engage one another in good faith that we will enter this perpetual life-cycle where the divine becomes human so that the human can become divine.

x X x

The liquid self: technology, Facebook, liquidity

We cannot sit in contemplation until we understand all there is to know about life. However, more extended periods of reflection have traditionally been part of key transitions in life. For example, for a long time university was the place where those privileged enough to get there could spend time in reflective study and discussion. This marked the beginning of adulthood; after leaving school-based education and before embarking on a career path, students could take stock and work out who they were and what they were going to be. A sense of the monastic still remains in our language: one 'goes up' to study at a university, as if ascending a mountain to think, and 'comes down' when graduating to rejoin society and begin one's 'ministry' – from the old French for 'service'.

More recently, people have opted for a gap year before going to university, perhaps as a reaction to universities becoming less of a place to reflect, and more of a place to be trained in a vocation – ready to 'come down' and rejoin the consumer society to begin one's shopping. Either way, the opportunity to stop and think for a while before beginning adult life proper has been an informal rite of passage. It's perhaps worrying then when those who have been involved in campus life for some time warn that students, on the cusp of adulthood, are affording themselves little time for reflection over the course of their studies.

Mark Edmundson, Professor of English at the University of Virginia, rightly sees university as a stepping-stone between the life our parents have created for us, to the life we are going to create for ourselves. But in order for this to happen for a student, he notes, 'she has to face brilliant antagonists. She has to encounter thinkers who see the world in different terms than she does.'[11]

Isn't this what Jesus did in the desert? Did he not pause to face a 'brilliant antagonist'? There is a long history of fables about kings who, tiring of their sycophantic court, dress up in disguise and go out among their subjects to work out what they really think of them. Isn't this what we see Jesus doing? The incarnation was God taking on 'the human dress', as Blake put it, getting into disguise to bypass all the 'yes-men' of the Pharisees and religious leadership to work out what was really happening on the ground. To escape the protection of heaven and face the antagonists, great and small.

In his analysis of the development of human civilisation, and the place of the human body within the various iterations of city that we have existed in, Richard Sennett bemoans the bodily passivity that has grown with our ever-increasingly comfortable lives: 'Without a disturbed sense of ourselves, what will prompt most of us – who are not heroic figures knocking on the doors of crackhouses – to turn outward toward each other, to experience the Other?'[12]

It is our antagonists that will provide this disturbance to our sense of ourselves. It is by cherishing opportunities to be challenged, to be removed from our bodily passivity and comfort, that we will find ourselves turned outward. This is why the incarnate God lands in a cave, in an animal feeder; divine empathy comes from his very human discomfort.

It is not just comfort but speed that prevents us from being disturbed. With no time to pause and reflect, we end up missing the chance to have our views about our selves changed. Another educationalist, Yale professor Anthony Kronman, published a book entitled *Education's End: Why our colleges and universities have given up on the meaning of life*, in which he argues that the essential Platonic question of 'how to live' has been completely lost in the mad rush to gain 'qualifications'.

Edmundson, like Kronman, is pessimistic about the numbers of students who get this experience, and writes eloquently about the breakneck speed at which his students now live. In an experiment in one of his lectures on Thoreau's thoughts on technology, he asked his class to think back to the day before and count up the *simultaneous places* they had been. Chatting on a mobile and skim-reading a book while browsing a website with the TV in the background and instant messaging three friends would make, say, seven 'places' they were at the same time. Most of the class reached at least this total, while some managed double figures! As he notes, 'it wouldn't take the Dalai Lama or Thoreau to assure them that anyone who is in seven places at once is not anywhere in particular – not present, not here now.'[13] He goes on to note that at student parties he had attended, 'about a fourth of the people have their cell phones locked to their ears. What are they doing? "They're talking to their friends." About? "About another party they might conceivably go to." '[14] Of course, the people at the other party are on their phones discussing another place they might prefer to be too . . .

This high-speed life, accelerated by wireless technologies, affords wonderful access to a huge array of possibilities, but these possibilities crowd our view, thicken the ground with constant new growth, and leave the clearing under threat from fast-growing shoots. The result, it seems, is a steady stream of proto-adults who have at best a far more complex sense of identity, and at worst, raging insecurities about who they are. As the British think tank the Institute of Public Policy Research has dubbed them, they are 'Freedom's Orphans' – a generation who have been gifted with more choices than any cohort before them, but who are 'more dependent on brands to give them a sense of what aspirations, values and possessions are important and acceptable'.[15] The increased anxiety that this generation feels is genuine: the average child in the US is more anxious than those who were actually in psychiatric care in the 1950s.[16]

Much has already been written about philosopher and sociologist Zygmunt Bauman's 'Liquid Modernity' thesis – the idea that the modern world of fixed identities and clear scientific facts has begun to liquefy, resulting in a world where truth and identity are far more difficult things to pin down. In his 2005 book on the same theme, *Liquid Life*, Bauman has gone on to explore what this might mean for everyday existence. The outlook is not optimistic.

> The ground on which our life prospects are presumed to rest is admittedly shaky – as are our jobs, and the companies that offer them, our partners and networks of friends, the standing we enjoy in wider society and the self-esteem and self-confidence that come with it . . . Instead of great expectations and sweet dreams, 'progress' evokes an insomnia full of nightmares of 'being left behind', of missing the train or falling out of a fast-accelerating vehicle.[17]

We should not then be surprised at, or too critical of, university students. Before having to enter the shaky and uncertain world proper, these few years are a welcome freedom, not to be spent in self-reflection, nor as opportunities to debate the grand ideas of life with antagonists. They are festival years, breathing spaces from the insecurities of life, opportunities to fraternise with as many people as possible, while drinking as much as possible in the process. 'Liquid' modernity indeed.[18]

It was out of this highly liquid (almost gaseous, nebulous, we might wonder?)[19] university scene that the social-networking site Facebook sprung. It still remains to be seen what long-term effect online 'social networks' will have on us as a society. Should Christians be celebrating the blossoming of a million online relationships, in prayerful awe at the gospel opportunities they hold? Or retreating in fear at the noisy chaos of it all, its unsupervised bawdiness and licentious temptations? In a liquid world where people's relationships are increasingly perceived as 'shaky', should we celebrate Facebook's ability to keep people connected, or be concerned that it is adding to the problem, and denigrating the idea of friendship? These are questions whose answers are not yet available to us, though some are suggesting that there could be very real dangers in our increasing reliance on digital relationships. Susan Greenfield, Professor of Synaptic Pharmacology in Oxford has warned that 'children's experiences on social networking sites are devoid of cohesive narrative and long-term significance. As a consequence, the mid-21st century mind might almost be infantilised, characterised by short attention spans, sensationalism, inability to empathise and a shaky sense of identity.'[20]

The key word here is 'might'. In discussions I have had with people on the subject, many have been keen to point out that adults *always* criticise the world that their children live in, whether it be punk music, clubbing or online gaming. What I think is interesting to ask though is whether we are witnessing something genuinely unprecedented. Perhaps the ability to represent ourselves remotely to a wide range of people whom we do not know face to face *is* new. If it is, then it is not enough simply to dismiss concerns as the usual fears of aging parents.[21]

In the summer of 2007 I signed up to Facebook, partly as I was going to be travelling to the US to promote a book, and it seemed like a good way to spread the word about it. Having done so, the first thing that struck me was the tantalising tsunami of possibilities. Everyone you have ever met may be out there. That girl at that party. That guy from school. They could be just a click away. This quickly led to a second realisation: I was going to have to create an online version of myself in my 'profile'. I had the option to say what music I liked, and to choose a photo of myself.

These profile photos are hugely interesting. Each has been chosen with care. What are they trying to say about us, what messages are they giving? In *Liquid Life*, Bauman talks of the 'mind boggling quandary' of having to mark oneself out as an individual, while also remaining obviously an acceptable part of the group. It is this tension that is displayed so clearly in so many profile photos: I am an individual – not like everyone else! – and, look at me, I'm an acceptable person – just like everyone else!

The online personae that we create on sites like Facebook are fantasy versions of ourselves. We are funnier than in real life, and better looking. We admit to liking certain forms of music, and claim to be reading books that perhaps we are not – ones that may impress people. It wasn't so long ago that the atom (from the Greek *α-τεμνω*, 'un-cuttable') was thought to be utterly indivisible, the basic unit of all matter. Now we have had to come to terms with the glorious complexities of its sub-atomic strangeness. Similarly, as we used to be able to look at ourselves as 'individuals' – the indivisible human unit, clearly labelled in its history, place and profession – we are now having to come to terms with the fracture of this atom too, with its multiple personalities created in myriad virtual worlds.

One of the questions this raises is whether Edmundson's students, existing in seven or more places at once, can really be called 'individuals' at all. Is there some irreducible 'Self' that exists coherent in all of these different versions of themselves that they – and we – are creating day by day as we surf the Internet, share our music on MySpace and video chat with people on the other side of the world?

Indeed, perhaps none of us should claim 'individuality'. A recent article in the US magazine *Atlantic* made the case for multiple selves actually being good science. As the blurb for the piece goes, 'an evolving approach to the science of pleasure suggests that each of us contains multiple selves – all with different desires, and all fighting for control'. This shouldn't surprise us, of course. Paul wrote of the compromised self, which cannot do what it knows it should, and yet does what it knows it shouldn't. The parallels continue as the article continues, though in rather less Pauline tones:

> Even if each of us is a community, all the members shouldn't get an equal say . . . We typically spend more of our lives not wanting to snort coke, smoke, or overeat than we spend wanting to do these things; this means that the long-term self has more time to reflect. It is less selfish; it talks to other people, reads books, and so on. And it tries to control the short-term

selves. As Jon Elster observes, the long-term, sober self is a truer self, because it tries to bind the short-term, drunk self. The long-term, sober self is the adult.[22]

So, while none of us could honestly claim individuality, becoming individual *is* a goal of the mature Self. 'Lord lead me,' as Paul Tillich prayed, 'from a life divided, to a life united.'

A recent advertising campaign for a telecoms company spun a different line. Hoardings announcing 'I am my older sister, I am my first car, I am all the girls I have kissed . . .' all ended with the strap-line 'I am who I am because of everyone.' There is something true in this: we are the sum of our influences and experiences. The question that I think remains is whether *mediated* connections with everyone around me – through text messages, Skype chats and other screen simulations – will lead me further towards mature unity, towards individuality, or divide me into ever shallower fractions.

The problem Moses faced when sent by God to save the Israelites in slavery is perhaps salient. 'Who shall I say sent me?' he asks, and perhaps the modern answer would have been for God to respond 'whoever they want me to be'; in a liberal democracy, 'God is who God is because of everyone.' But this would not do, and in what may be taken as a radical critique of both the complex and confused sense of who the Israelites thought they were after so much suffering and oppression, and of our own very liquid identities, God tells Moses simply to say that the 'I AM' sent him, a robust statement of the divine individuality – an unbreakable, irreducible self which is our aspiration.

Our spirits may still call for it, but our screen-fixed eyes appear less keen. As society has 'atomised' (and perhaps Michael Houellebeq didn't go far enough with his metaphor in his novel of that name) so we have atomised too. What is not quite clear yet is whether our retreat from physical connections – from communities identified by physical proximity rather than interest group – will have a wider impact on our society. That we are retreating is quite clear: gated communities are becoming more and more common, and home security is a top priority. Our cars are almost like armoured vehicles now; we drive our children around in them to protect them, worried that if they walk to school they will be 'got'.

While the causality is by no means established, it does appear ironic that the huge blossoming in 'friendship' – as defined by Facebook – has been paralleled by increases in teenage violent crime. We can't yet say whether the retreat into the relative safety of online worlds like Second Life is causing people to fear the physical presence of 'the other', or if time spent in these worlds means people deal with negotiating differences with 'the other' less well. (The causality may be the reverse: increasingly violent city life is pushing people into the risk-free interactions offered by online life.) Certainly, for web commentators like Geert Lovink, our herd movement from MySpace to Facebook to Twitter and on to the inevitable next thing suggests we are yearning for more:

> Networking sites are social drugs for those in need of the Human that is located elsewhere in time or space. It is the pseudo Other that we are connecting to. Not the radical Other or some real Other. We systematically explore weakness and vagueness and are pressed to further enhance the exhibition of the Self. 'I might know you (but I don't). Do you mind knowing me?'[23]

I think this is a too-harsh critique, and as a regular user of various social networks I can attest to them being a really positive and interesting way to communicate with others. For every time they are used to retreat from life, there are other examples where they have drawn people out into the city to get involved in events or campaigns.

Either way, what is clear from the ever-increasing levels of security – from CCTV to gated communities to SUVs and firewalls – is that in the words of the *Hedgehog Review*, 'in the absence of existential comfort, we have now come to settle for safety, or the pretence of safety'.[24] And we have done so through the deployment of machines.

Jesus' walking into the desert was a deliberate act against settling for safety. He knew, as so many before and after in so many traditions have found, that in order to see more clearly who we are at the core of ourselves, we need to step out of comfort, step out of safety and into the deserts – the fasting places. The prophet who turned water into wine goes there to *not* drink, the generous provider who shared loaves and fish to feed thousands goes there to *not* eat, to not consume, to not buy or sell or text or call or update his profile, in order to allow the waters from which he has just risen, baptised and affirmed by God, to settle, that he may better look and see clearly just who he is.

In other words, though we shouldn't attempt to live there, we do regularly need to go to the desert to escape the machines; to go to remind ourselves that, despite our now inextricable reliance on digital telecommunications, combustion engines and synthetic chemistry, we are not, at our core, automata. Perhaps this is what our Sabbath should be: a day to turn off.

Writing on the limitations of technology, Ivan Illich, the radical Marxist critic of technology and education, noted that 'only within limits can machines take the place of slaves; beyond these limits they lead to a new type of serfdom'.[25] Commenting on this, Aaron Falbel writes that 'Genuinely human acts have more and more been replaced by the operation of machines, institutions and systems. Everything from procuring the food we eat to dealing with the excrement we leave behind, from birthing to dying, from healing to moving – has been designed, rationalised, engineered . . .'[26]

I think these are powerful words for us to reflect on and respond to as we head further into universal wireless access and always-on connectivity. We need to be better aware of our co-evolution with our devices. We make them, but they are also remaking us – and in the worse cases this can lead to a chronic shallowing of the self.

I have often been to church gatherings where, in a room full of people, there is virtually nobody there. There are people in the room, but with their Macs open or their gazes focused on Blackberrys and iPhones, they are mentally elsewhere. It appears to be a kind of defence mechanism: if I were to commit to being fully present in this space I would have to be responsible for it, and deal with what is being said. But if I remove my attention a little . . .

It is no different to the sorts of workplaces many of us inhabit, modern offices so brilliantly satirised in Joshua Ferris' novel *And Then We Came to the End*, 'a story about sitting all morning next to someone you deliberately cross the road to avoid at lunchtime'. Indeed, it is in these spaces, fictional or real, that I have most understood Illich's words about 'a new type of serfdom'. We are not surfing the net; it is 'serfing' us. Emails are delivered immediately, and must be dealt with now; news can be accessed in real time, and must be kept abreast of; the hundreds in my social networks can be told what I am doing now, and now, and now, and *need* to be told now – lest I get left behind. The result? We have no time for the other, not while we must quickly chomp down our chicken and salsa wrap. The project of building and maintaining our myriad digital fantasy selves simply leaves no time for it.

All of us soon realise this is a soul-destroying situation to be in. Arguing against the modern atheist polemic, the agnostic journalist Roger Scruton recently wrote in the British political monthly *Prospect* that 'religion is not primarily about God, but about the human need for the sacred'. As to what the sacred might be, he defined it as 'moments that stand outside time, in which the loneliness and anxiety of the human individual is confronted and overcome, through immersion in the group'.[27]

We are all crying out for these moments of inclusion and immersion, but our mistake is to believe that technology alone will bring them to us, and will rid us of loneliness and anxiety.

Let us be clear: I am not a Luddite, condemning technological progress out of hand. I use Facebook myself, have been a

41

prolific blogger, and am a regular Twitter user. But, while they undoubtedly make some form of connection between us, I remain sceptical about their ability to get to the heart of our human need to be present, to experience presence with others. They can facilitate these connections, but they do not themselves provide them, and it is a failure to understand this subtle distinction that I fear leaves many existing as 'hungry ghosts', suffering profound web-loneliness. As we have seen, behind the constantly cheery updates (and by all measures self-confidence is increasing in the population) a defence mechanism can lurk that involves self-promotion and ego-building, but masks a core low self-esteem. We feel less secure, so shore up our confidence with lots of photos of us out at bars and events, and lots of cheerful web-chatter.

To return to Sartre, what all of our tools do, whether flint arrows, ploughs or notebooks, is exaggerate the paradox of our identity as both facticity and transcendence. With these exaggerations come huge positives, on both sides. Those with physical disabilities are using virtual worlds like Second Life to transcend – if only virtually – the facts of their limited physical movement. The democratisation of technology has also been hugely positive for many creative industries. Budding musicians now no longer have to rely on the rare blessing of music labels to have their work released. The danger of the exaggeration, however, is that the potential to collapse this paradox of who we are is also heightened. It is now far easier to present ourselves, or see others, as a flattened image of status updates and short soundbites. It is also far easier to flee the facts of our situation – disappointment, poverty, loneliness – and blindly attempt to transcend them in virtual worlds without due thought for the reality of our lives.

So while we must not be seen as technophobes, nor as those who are against technology as a tool for enriching our relationships, we must also not be seen as uncritical or ignorant of the potential pitfalls, both psychologically and physiologically, which an unreflective use of technology could lead to.

To use another metaphor, presented by the philosopher Manuel de Landa, we need to carefully examine whether the wireless, always-on, digital self will turn out to be *endoskeletal* or *exoskeletal*. Technologies are no more than tools that, like the skeletons we have evolved over the millennia, allow us to function in new ways. Organisms with an endoskeleton – an internal bone structure – are given a whole new level of motion control. They can run, hold, flex and stand. It may be that the Internet will give us new ways in which to move, new internal structures that will radically affect the ways in which we can hold one another. But de Landa sees some technologies – like the early walled cities – as exoskeletal. They are protective, tortoise-like shells within which people can safely grow and prosper without fear of attack. They are places to withdraw to when the other threatens, and, while offering security, make animals slow and unresponsive. As people withdraw behind firewalls and screens into anodyne and sterile – but perfectly secure – worlds, it may be that the Internet will lead us away from any genuine interaction with the other, and simply seal us in our shells.

The reality will doubtless lie somewhere in between. The 'liquid self' is an inherently flexible self, fitting in to new situations, and assimilating new technologies. This is to be celebrated. In a fast-changing world we need to be adaptive, open to our environment, and with permeable borders ready to sense the other. But the liquid self is also a fearful self. So concerned as it is not to offend anyone, or to appear exclusive, or to find itself excluded, it ends up atomised, dissolved into solution and disappearing.

The self that has dissolved into a Facebook world is useless to anyone. Without conviction, without a proper backbone, our bodies slump to the floor, unable to hold any position. The antagonist questions us, but we refuse to give any answer. The church, the Internet, our mobile, our multiple online selves, become protective covers, hardened smokescreens behind which we can keep our real thoughts obscured.

It is in the clearing, in the desert, Sabbath spaces which we carry with us that we will gain 'passage to those beings that we ourselves are not, and access to the being that we ourselves are'. I have been to the deserts around Jerusalem. They are open places, without shelter, in which nothing can hide. So much of our lives are spent in front of a screen; we must learn to see that this simultaneously places us behind a screen too. These LCD windows can be dark glasses behind which we hide ourselves, behind which we duck questions from the antagonist. There comes a time when we must log-off, unplug and fast – withdraw from connection in order to become a better agent of connection when we return.

Ironically then, perhaps it is in the clearing that we find we have no signal. This is a good place to be for a while. Go there.

Small screen communion

iPod, phone
held close
and thumbed,
illuminating so dimly
the lichened branches
fingering the above,
are such small lights
on these paths
at night.

What possible guidance
could they offer?
Yet still
I look,
still we look
so intently
at their ever-decreasing thinness
and ask of them
the same
as wafers
once gave.

x X x

The narrated self: story, infantilism, heroism

Whether it is our real thoughts or just temporary fictions, blogs, social networks and sites like Twitter all appear to have one major strand running through them: personal narrative. Whether in 140 characters as in Twitter, or in photos as on Flickr, or through regular posting on blogs, 'Web 2.0' has been about user-generated content: it allows us to tell our story.

This is a wonderful thing. The democratisation of publishing is hugely positive for society, and should, we hope, lead to improved transparency in governance, and less abuse of human rights. What is interesting is the timing of the rise in 'micro-narrative' technologies like blogs and Twitter in these liquid modern times, which coincides precisely with the collapse of traditional 'meta-narratives' in the 'solid modern' times that have passed. In other words, when the grand narratives disintegrated, it wasn't that story went with them. On the contrary, more and more smaller stories began to be told to fill the void. As human beings we have an innate need for story in our lives, and the large singular mass of meta-narrative has been replaced by the smaller multiple masses of the micro-stories we tell each day. The liquid self may be a permanent shape-shifter, but it is also a great story-maker, and technology has given us the tools to un-gag the narrated self.

So what is it is about stories that make them so central to our existence? In his comprehensive volume on the subject, Christopher Booker draws an interesting conclusion. All stories are based around the idea, corrupted or otherwise, of a hero or heroine. But, as he explains, the roots of those two words are a mystery:

> After many years working on this book, I am convinced that, lost in the mists of history, the [word hero] must be closely related in some way to our word 'heir'. In other words, the hero

or heroine is he or she who is born to inherit; who is worthy to succeed; who must grow up as fit to take on the torch of life from those who went before. Such is the essence of the task laid on each of us as we come into this world. That is what stories are trying to tell us.[28]

We tell stories because we are trying, together, in those shared moments of narrative, to work out how to become 'worthy to succeed'. This is why the hero and heroine are said to 'live happily ever after' – because they have reached a place of succession, where they have carried the torch successfully, and now hand it on to their own children, who must, in turn, struggle with it.

It is the beginnings of this struggle to become the hero that we see in Jesus' time in the desert. What sort of hero is he going to become? The vain, self-obsessed, violent, tragic figure whose life, in the classic arc of stories, must end in death? Or the truly 'heroic' figure who gives his life for others, and yet lives on?

Later in the Gospels, Jesus tells a story about two sons, both of whom act out heroic roles in different ways. The younger son is brash and wants the high life. In an act that suggests he wished his father was dead, he asks for his inheritance but, not yet being the mature self ready to inherit, squanders it in fast living. In the meantime, the other son is hard working and desperate to please. He is a different sort of hero: the reliable son who will graft to earn his father's favour.

While the traditional telling of this 'return of the prodigal son' concentrates on the younger son's excesses, and uses the story as a warning against wild behaviour, the real meaning appears to be more complex. In his wonderful book of reflections on Rembrandt's depiction of the moment of return, Henri Nouwen tracks his discovery of being like both the younger son, wild and rebellious, and the elder, litigious and conservative and in fear of an angry God-Father. He finally realises however that, 'though I am both the younger son and the elder son, I am not to remain them, but to become the Father'.[29]

Both sons had to overcome their failings, their insecurities, their depressions and doubts; both had to go beyond being heroes – whether that meant living the playboy life or being so proud of their faithfulness – to become 'heirs' to their true inheritance. We are fooled into thinking that the money was the inheritance that the father had to pass on, but it was not. His real gift was his love and acceptance. 'Simply accept,' Paul Tillich has written, 'the fact that you are accepted.'

The fact that we are accepted is the hard and often painful truth we must come to terms with before we are ready to move into adulthood. Is it too much to suggest that, having been told at his baptism that he was accepted by God, it was into the desert to struggle with this truth that Jesus went?

This move from childish heroism to adulthood is neither easy, and nor is it much encouraged. The humourist Michael Bywater has recently written a book called *Big Babies*, in which he argues that we have been reduced to permanent infantilism, prevented from becoming adults by our consumer culture. He summarises his thesis thus:

> You are surrounded by an ocean of voices speaking to you in baby-talk, and here is a random sample of what they think of you; of all of us:
> - we have no discrimination,
> - we are unable to control our appetites,
> - we cannot postpone gratification,
> - we have little sense of self, and what we do have is deformed.[30]

It is a witty book with a serious point: we need to grow up, but consumerism would prefer us to remain clueless infants. In contrast to this, fasting in the desert, we find that it is precisely in a display of gratification postponement, of appetite control and discrimination that Jesus finds his sense of self. This is the moment in which he begins the journey from simply being the son to becoming one with the Father.

Unless we are prepared to negotiate a similar journey to that of Christ, we are destined to remain but children. Nouwen makes it clear: 'No father or mother ever became father or mother without having been son or daughter, but every son and daughter has to consciously choose to step beyond their childhood *and become father and mother for others*.'[31] This is why we must begin with the self, because it is only if we are able to find a secure sense of who we are that we will be able to engage with the other in a way that is not child-like. 'It is a hard and lonely step,' Nouwen goes on, 'especially in a period of history in which parenthood is so hard to live well – but it is a step that is essential for the fulfilment of the spiritual journey.'[32] Fulfilment meaning, if we read both lines together, becoming father and mother to others – being ones who can help 'others' to battle with their own selves and come to a place of fulfilment too.[33]

This is, of course, not about becoming parents *per se*. Nouwen was a Catholic priest with a complex sexuality who knew that, while he must 'become the father', he would probably never have children himself. Yet while he never became a biological father, he was truly a parent to many, especially those in the L'Arche community around the world.

As a parent myself, I have begun to know something of the change in life that parenthood brings; it essentially boils down to having to look out for someone other than yourself.[34] As my young son and daughter bring me ridiculous hats and ties to wear, and drag me to day-glo playgrounds, I wonder now if this willingness to let those in our care playfully control us is partly what Jesus meant when he spoke to Peter after the resurrection: 'I tell you the truth, when you were younger you dressed yourself and went where you wanted; but when you are old you will stretch out your hands, and someone else will dress you and lead you where you do not want to go' (John 21:18). Peter the childish, impetuous disciple, was going to have to grow up and become the Pope – the 'Papa', as the Italians still have it – the father of the Church. He would no longer be totally in control.

49

This is the archetypal plot for every narrated self. Point by point, word by word, post by post, we are telling the story of our selves, all with the background and back story of those who created us and those with whom we share episodes and vignettes. Within each of these stories there will be ruptures and pauses, and in our reflections on 'what kind of selves we need to be in order to live in harmony with others' it is important for us to occasionally stop both reading and writing and consider the direction we are taking our tales.

Peter's own story was full such ruptures: here was a fisherman who dropped everything to follow Jesus, a disciple who dropped his sword and ran away in denial, a humbled friend, forgiven – then put in charge of the fledgling community of believers, a Jew forced to accept God's acceptance of non-Jews.

As we will see, Peter's is a story of the hero, the strong-minded, fiery-tempered idealist, becoming the heir, but it is here that we need to probe Booker's concept of the 'hero' and the 'heir' more carefully. He equates the words – their meanings are intertwined together in the mists of the past – but I think it may be more accurate to make a subtle distinction between them.

In the classic arc of a story we leave the hero 'living happily ever after' – very often at the wedding of the hero and some princess. Their struggle is over – they have overcome much and learned a great deal. They are now, in this last moment, and *only* at this last moment, the heir. So the majority of stories leave us on the cusp of in-heir-itance: the hero married and living happily with the rich king, but not having actually yet become the king themselves. Whether they will go on to take the inheritance, and to pass it on, is another story. For Booker, being an heir is simply a temporary state between heroism and Nouwen's 'parenthood'.

Zygmunt Bauman analyses heroes from a different angle. For him, the archetypal heroes are those who died gloriously for their country, in the age when nations were being formed: 'The era of nation-state building had to be a time of heroism, of heroic patriotism, to be precise.'[35] In this way, heroism 'used to be measured by the number of enemies which the hero's suicide destroyed'.[36] In Bauman's usage, the hero cannot become the heir, because the hero always dies for the cause, and takes many enemies down with them in the fight. Samson is the classic example here (see Judg. 16:30).

Against the hero, Bauman sets up the archetype of the martyr. The martyr dies at the hand of enemies, like the hero, but dies without causing death. Instead, their singular death is punishment by the enemy for sticking unswervingly to the truth: 'Accepting martyrdom, the prospective victims cannot be sure that their death will indeed promote that cause and help to make its triumph certain . . . The best martyrs could hope for was the ultimate proof of their own moral probity; heroes on the other hand, are modern – they calculate gains and losses, they want their sacrifice repaid.'[37]

Bauman locates the age of martyrs as biblical times, and the age of the heroes as the period of nation building – leading up to modern times. Both of them were fundamental to the narratives of the societies that hosted them. What has superseded both of them in the Liquid World – which has no need for martyrs or heroes – is the celebrity. (Though it is interesting to note that we still seem to require our celebrities to suffer – sending them into the 'desert' in programmes like *I'm A Celebrity Get Me Out of Here*, or humiliating them in telethons.)

This move from martyr to celebrity, through hero, is one of increased focus on the ego. The martyr dies, but solely for the cause; the hero dies, but in a blaze of glory; the celebrity takes the glory and remains in living death – using surgery to refuse all signs of aging.

As we look at Peter, we can now pause to wonder what sort of death he aimed at. What sort of self was he going to be? Would he be the hero, in Bauman's sense, dying for the cause and drawing his sword and taking everyone with him? He certainly dodged his first opportunity to be a martyr, denying he even knew Jesus, and thus letting his principles buckle. Once restored, he sets out on the more complex path: the natural hero instinct within him is tempered by his realisation that he has been appointed an heir, father of the church – though what is interesting now is how his position of 'Papa' has been twisted into that of an unimpeachable, undying, ever-renewing celebrity.

As emerging 'narrated selves' in a digital world, as small societies constantly under construction, we must, like Peter, always be prepared for the rupture of having to move from heroism, with the ego at the fore, to heir-ism, becoming father and mother to others. In a sense, our time spent in reflection, in *Lichtung*, is preparation for what our reflex responses will be when these ruptures occur.

It is interesting to note how, in their moments of crisis Judas and, I believe, Paul, showed very different reflexes to those Jesus displayed. Judas' act of betrayal can be seen as his attempt to catalyse a political revolution. As a zealot Judas knew that this would very probably lead to some violence and death – but these fallen would be heroes, dying and killing for a political cause. Judas sees Jesus as potentially powerful, but needing someone to light the touch paper. He thus reacts to the dramatic turn of events as they come to Jerusalem for the Passover with an eye for strategy: he will take control of the narrative and become its hero, even as he promotes Jesus as that hero figure. He fails of course; Jesus will not have his death politicised, will not be that ego-centric hero.

Like Judas, I think we can see something of the strategist in Paul too. In a very similar way to Jesus he decides, against other people's advice, that the time was right for him to go to Jerusalem (see Acts 21). It is there that, just as Jesus was, he is arrested on blasphemy charges after a disturbance at the temple. Both were harassed by a large crowd, and both hauled before hearings of Jewish and Roman officials.

It is almost as if Paul was trying to follow in Jesus' footsteps – and perhaps even trying to do better than Jesus had, for, once arrested, his and Jesus' actions diverge dramatically. Jesus says virtually nothing, and does nothing to defend himself, whereas

Paul, never short of words, never seems to *stop* talking. He preaches to the crowds, he creates a defence at his hearings and never fails to hammer home his credentials: a Jew thoroughly trained in the law, a Roman citizen. He appears to get angry and insults the High Priest, without even knowing who he is (Acts 23:4–5). He is then taken to another hearing where he 'appeals to Caesar' and demands to be sent to Rome.

I wonder if this is Paul the strategist at work. Just as Judas had tried to wrestle control of the narrative and become the hero, so Paul does everything he can in order to get himself to Rome, the power base of the known world. He had tried to do so on many previous occasions, but had been foiled by weather and other events. Now he manufactures a situation which he knows will get him there, even if it is in chains. He knows he will be jailed, and probably killed – but not as a silent martyr, no. He will go as the hero, a sacrifice for the establishment of a strong Christian nation.[38]

It is strange to me that Paul was following Jesus' footsteps so closely, but then chose to react so differently. Why didn't he follow his Master's example and remain silent before his accusers? Is it unfair to see some of Bywater's childishness in his faith? His trip to Jerusalem was certainly for good reason – to support the poverty-stricken believers there – but it seems that there may have been ulterior motives too. Perhaps this is the thorn in Paul's flesh – his strategist's heart, his desire to be at the centre of the action, the hero. Much later, as he writes of this to his 'children in Corinth' – after imprisonments, after much hardship, after years more maturing thought, he now won't boast of anything other than weakness. The hero has again become the heir.

From Samson, through prodigals, Judas, Peter, Paul – and so to us. Like them, we are constantly engaged in the construction of our selves, constantly narrating the truths and fictions which make up who we are, and who others perceive us to be. This has always been the case. The digital revolution has simply multiplied the issues by a huge factor, and, in parallel, the mini-ruptures, the opportunities we have for moving our story in different ways have become more numerous.

What our times of *Lichtung* must do, our moments in the light, in the desert with our antagonists, stripped of our devices, is prepare us to steer the plot away from heroism, away from elevation of the ego, and towards becoming a true heir: passing on something of the divine Other to the others we meet on our journey. Like Judas and Paul, we will be tempted to strategise, especially those of us in positions of leadership. Like Peter and Samson we will be tempted to play the hero.

Like Jesus, like Mary, we must resist these positions. Never coming across as heroic, a suffering martyr or celebrity mum, Mary takes on her role as a 'womb of the divine' with grace and humility. She is the girl become parent, giving birth to newness, opening the way for change, responding only with her Magnificat.

Her son Jesus had the same identity struggles as the other men around him. Should he play the hero? Would his life be wasted in martyrdom? If he accepted that God had accepted him, could he grow up into divine parenthood himself?

We too are forgiven, accepted. We too are wombs of the divine. We too have been blessed with some gift, some service which we can give away to the heirs we allow to mature after us. We too have some gospel being written, some text under construction about us. Like all good stories, it will be a narrative that is punctuated by ruptures, but how we deal with those times, whether they lead us to maturity or fantasy, will be governed by the strength and focus we find in the desert we carry with us.

The maturing self: initiation, Pharisees, excursion

We are called to move from childhood to adulthood, and it is in the desert with our antagonists rather than searching with our machines, that this journey will begin. Quite when it will begin will be different for different people. But begin it must if we are ever to become mature people, mature communities who are able to relate peacefully with others.

James Fowler has written extensively about the maturing that occurs within spirituality in his 'stages of faith' model. This consists of six stages, which range from childish ideas of God and faith (like Santa Claus) through the third stage of external-ised authority structures (I believe because the Bible/my pastor teaches it) and into the conjunctivity and universality of the latter stages.[39] I strongly believe that if we are ever to see a properly functioning 'emergent' church, then it will have to be one fully conscious of these stages, and well set up to allow and encourage people to negotiate the paths between them. These churches will be recognised as generous places, while also being labelled 'dirty' by those who equate doctrinal purity with closeness to God.

A different perspective on the same essential journey of matu-ration is that of the 'two halves of life', separated by some kind of public ritual which displays our movement from the first to the second half. This same basic journey is undertaken in virtu-ally every culture on earth. Young men from the Maasai undergo circumcision as part of their initiation into adulthood, Bar Mitzvahs perform a similar function for Jews, and Australian Aboriginal boys spent months preparing for their full entry into society, with sacrifices and lessons on tribal law all part of the process. For some Christian groups baptism serves this purpose, and for some parts of groups like the Amish, this may be preceded by a period of 'rumspringa', where adolescents actually leave the community for a period to experience 'English' life – with all its sex, drugs and rock 'n roll – before returning and taking up full membership of the church.

We can see an archetype here: it is precisely in the time around puberty, when we gain the biological ability to reproduce and become parents, that all cultures and faiths seem to demand a period of 'excursion', a time away from the host community, often in physically demanding conditions, to prepare themselves for the task of parenthood. As we have seen, this is the plot of countless movies and books, from Austen to Dickens: a young girl looking for her prince (or vice versa) must undergo a journey of sorts, a rupture, a move away from the family home, facing all sorts of trials before returning triumphantly and enjoying a wonderful wedding.

The gospel makes interesting reading through this prism: Jesus is born in miraculous circumstances and then, at a particular time in his life, leaves home, undertakes a journey with a band of followers, is frustrated, suffers, leaves the reader under the impression that he has died, but then comes back victorious to await his 'bride'.

Within this narrative framework we can see Jesus' time in the desert in a new way. This is no longer the boy saying with innocent certainty that his parents could hardly expect to find him anywhere other than in the temple courts, in his Father's house. This is the man who now has no place to lay his head. His journey has begun. The first half of his life is over, and he must now begin the second.

'Desert' moments like these are always a powerful part of any story. This is where our hero – the heir-to-be – steps away from comfort and sees clearly the mission that is ahead of them. We see Frodo leaving the Shire, Telemachus leaving Ithaca, Dorothy stepping out onto the Yellow Brick Road, Lucy pushing aside the fur coats in the wardrobe and feeling the cold air of Narnia. All of these scenes are performed by characters on the cusp of adulthood, moving gently into the second half of life.

The monk Richard Rohr has spent a great deal of time exploring the idea of life having two halves. To condense his hypothesis dramatically: the first half of life is ideally spent training for the journey that will be undertaken and, as such, will be bound by all sorts of rules and regimes and drills. It is only once these rules have been internalised that we can begin the journey, to step outside of the drills into the real world and become responsible adults.

I see this process happening all the time in my teaching. When students first arrive in my classes at the school, I am very strict about punctuality, about handing homework in on time, about ruling each page with a margin and being precise working things out. It is a very different story for my older classes. Of course, I fully expect them to be on time and to produce high quality work, but by the time they are entering the final couple of years of school, I expect them to have internalised these rules and understand *why* they are important in ways that younger students simply cannot do. In this sense, if they then chose to break them, the responsibility for the consequences is fully theirs: poor grades. But they cannot be given this responsibility from day one.

Every parent knows this is true. We begin with hard and fast rules: *never* play with knives, *never* speak to strangers, *never* run across the road – and rightly so. But it would be idiocy to claim these as unchangeable laws that should go on forever. All adults need to be able to handle knives, speak to strangers, and dodge cars in the city traffic.

Rohr notes that Paul takes chapters upon chapters in Romans to say the same thing, while the Dalai Lama is more succinct: 'we must learn the Law very well, in order to know how to break it properly.' The first half of life is thus about learning obedience and duty, and what is right and wrong. Our games in childhood are clear cut: Cowboys and Indians, the Rebellion vs the Empire. It is a time for being a good Boy Scout, for knowing exactly who the goodies are.

As Freud would have it, we need the boundaries and rules of the first half in order to create a secure ego-structure. But the whole reason for the creation of this structure is that we might then be able to move from it and ask the right sorts of questions. One of the key problems we face, according to Rohr, is that so much of our political and religious leadership has consisted of men who have never got beyond this first half. Despite being mature in years, they *still* see things as absolutely clear cut, still see the world in terms of an axis of evil and still see religion in terms of dirty and clean, in and out. Healthy as it is to have a well-bounded first half of life, it is profoundly unhealthy to retain those views late on in life.

Creating a secure ego but never moving beyond it is one problem. But, equally unhealthy, and equally common now, is growing up with no rules or boundaries to facilitate the creation of a secure self. Children, I have often mused as a teacher, are like a gas: they will expand to fill whatever boundaries you give them. (One wonders if Bauman will have to develop a theory of 'gaseous modernity' if the infantile leanings of society get stronger.) Every class I have ever taught is the same: they kick and push the boundaries until they find something solid, immoveable, and then relax back, happy that they have established where they are and the space they have. My job in the first few weeks then is to maintain tight boundaries. If I can do that for six weeks, then they'll probably give me very little trouble for the rest of the year.

Jesus clearly spent much of his youth learning the Jewish law, and learning it very well. His knowledge of it amazed even the leading teachers of the day. But it would have been no gospel if he had simply gone about preaching adherence to the law. It was precisely because he had *internalised* the law, and was preaching about life *beyond* it that he was crucified. The Jewish religious establishment were stuck in the first half of life, and did not like one bit this well-versed, secure radical who knew the tradition as well as they did, but was living a life beyond its dead regulation.

Returning to Paul, we see a similar story. He is a 'Pharisee, the son of a Pharisee' who is extremely well versed in the law. Yet, while this serves him very well in the first half of life, it is causing much pain and suffering to others in the second. His blinkered views, his insistence on the purity of his faith, his arrogance about what is right and wrong, good and evil, is leading to people being hunted down and killed. But God has other plans for Paul. He strikes him blind, and leads him into new places, based on grace, not the law. Interestingly, Paul initially experienced this rupture as heresy: he was being asked to believe things that he considered utterly wrong, and to associate with those he considered heretical. As we shall see later, these divine interruptions are often highly challenging to the orthodoxy we have grown accustomed to, and can be mediated by people – tricksters, heretics, pirates – that we consider to be shockingly out of line. It took Paul quite some time before grace was fully dominant in his life – and one might posit that the harder tone of his earlier letters shows that he was still struggling with first-half sensibilities well after his conversion.

Bringing some of these strands together it seems perhaps that there is a parallel to be drawn between Bauman and Booker's figures of the hero, and the devoted Pharisee straining to be perfect under the law. Pre-Damascus, Paul was working very hard to be a Jewish hero. He was upholding the law, fighting and slaying to secure the walls of Judaism. This hero-spirit, controlled by the ego, appears to have lived on a little in him and his high-energy missionary activity. But, as he grows as a Christian, he knows this spirit has to die. He must 'die to the law' – the heroic, egotistical self – and allow Christ the heir to be reborn in him. The legal Paul dies; it is grace that sustains him now and his concern is more for parenting the churches he has planted, just as in the Old Testament Elijah, the prophet of the law, disappears into the desert, leaving his cloak and aura to Elisha, the 'prophet of grace'.[40]

It is this same grace that best exemplifies the spirit of the father in the story of the prodigal son. Gracious, generous grace – the gift that is outside the exchange of commodities, outside the hero's economy of gains and losses, of earned righteousness – is the soul bequest of the heir, of those moving in the second half of life.

So, as we move from childhood to adulthood, through Fowler's stages of faith, taking moments in *Lichtung* to reflect and be questioned, we must keep in mind this arc of our journey: a movement away from heroism, away from dying for causes at all, towards being good heirs.

This will be painful, as the father found out, agreeing as he did to his young son's request for 'rumspringa'. It will also be painful as we watch our elder sons become legalistic, trying to be heroes in an entirely different way, and criticising us for our woolly liberalism. But if we are to be good parents, good leaders, we must accept these reactions from our maturing children, and wait patiently for both of them, just as God has waited for us.

The second half of life is the life of the father, the parent. To the young, it may seem that life is over by this point. Our parents are boring and square. They don't have the radical energy and iconoclasm of their children. It will be painful, I imagine, to hear my children say this. And, I realise now, it must have been painful for my parents to hear it from me. But, I begin to see now, it is only in the move towards the individuality, the security and maturity of the second half of life, that we begin to begin to 'become the sorts of selves that can live in harmony with others'. At the same time, I see that there are still many dark nights to be navigated, many hours spent awake waiting, before the legal self dies, and grace begins to move in me.

Stones

If we could all
just stop throwing stones,
and stoop, knees bent
and write in the dust,

we'd see that the dust
was once stone –
grand, and hard, and proud, and tough –
now ground and dissolved
in grace and tears.

So . . . how much better
to be a grain of dirt
on that kind prophet's hands
than a stone
in the cold, accusing Temple
of the pure.

x X x

The obscured self: darkness, mundanity, blindness

> One does not discover new lands without consenting to lose sight of the shore for a very long time. (André Gide)

Paul's blinding conversion and Jesus' time in the desert are both examples of radical entries into Heidegger's 'clearing', of coming upon the truer core of ourselves and the different light that illuminates us there. They are, in the fullest sense, moments of enlightenment. Yet, strangely, they are also within the corpus of what have become known as 'dark nights of the soul'.[41] Gazing fully into the light can be blinding, as the poet Don Paterson has reflected; 'we turn from the light to see'.[42]

We see these moments of darkness used as devices in so many stories: blindness has long been an affliction of the best prophets and seers. For those struck blind temporarily, thrown into darkness and soul-searching, the night, like the clearing, is another opportunity for enlightenment, or, to be more precise, an opportunity to mourn the light that has gone out, and thus grow fonder for its return. As Booker would have it, the night is entered by the proud protagonist, but dawn comes to the humbled hero – the heir to be.

Strange things happen in the dark. Once our eyes get used to the shadows, our rational minds work hard to create sense of the trickle of visual information. They conjure *nyktomorphs* – 'night-shapes' – suddenly making monsters out of hedgerows, and rifles from branches, deliberately running riot in our hippocampus, the ancient animal core of the brain, wanting us to get up and flee the danger of the night.

It is in these dark nights that our first-half-of-life views are put to the test. Having got used to things being so black and white, having become so used to Scripture making perfect sense, we are then plunged into darkness. The light is switched off; in the middle of the afternoon, the sun goes out.

This was Job's experience. For no apparent reason he was plunged into suffering, disease and poverty. What would his response be? He was tempted by those who came to him in the darkness of his night to curse God, or find some root cause for his affliction and be done with it. Job refused, and we see this same refusal to curse the darkness in Jesus' passion, as he too is utterly abandoned by God. He asks only one question of his Father's desertion: why?

In an inversion of the usual reading of this passion narrative, Žižek notes that it is at this precise moment of abandonment that Jesus becomes most fully human, and God 'stumbles upon the limit of his omnipotence'. Thus, in our own moments of darkness, 'at that very moment of the utmost abjection, I am absolutely close to God, since I find myself in the position of the abandoned Christ . . . Man's identity with God is asserted only in/through God's radical self-abandonment.'[43]

Though we must not love the darkness, we must also not run from it. If at all we can we must sit patiently, like Job, and reflect on the paradox of abandonment and communion, for it is in these moments that we begin to better appreciate the gentle clarity of the 'clearing' and how we should treasure it when it returns.

It is also here that the work of preparing us to engage with the other is done. If it is in our darkest moments that we are closest to God, then what unites all of humanity, what binds me inextricably to the other, is this shared and most basic experience of abandonment and suffering. Too often dialogue between religions has focused on what common ideas about God people can share, or what universal values we can uphold. If Žižek is right, then it is the universal experience of suffering and oppression that may well provide the most fertile soil for discussion, for 'what unites us is the same struggle'.[44]

We will all face the darkness at some point, and we need all to see the great tradition of growth in the dark that we belong to.

Paul was blinded, Jesus abandoned in the dark, and we will join them. But, as we do so, we must beware the *nyktomorphs* that will creep up on us, try to scare us, tell us to move on, and demand that lights are lit. Those who have been through dark nights will know this temptation to chase the darkness with artificial light, and one of the things we must be aware of with technology is the temptation to use it in this way. Back-lit computer screens and 42-inch plasma televisions are the ever-on lanterns that promise us escape from whatever darkness, loneliness or abandonment we feel. These are not promises that they can keep.

Job's darkness, and the experiences of Paul and others can be seen as short bursts of intense blinding. The suffering is great, but may not last long. Yet this is not always the case. Richard Rohr draws heavily on the work of the psychiatrist and theologian Gerald May, who explored deeply the concept of the dark night of the soul. What Rohr makes clear from May's work is that the traditional view of the 'dark night' of St John of the Cross and others being a time of immense suffering is not always correct. The darkness is not so much an oppression of evil, but more a hiding, an obscuring of God and meaning, as hinted at in the original Spanish *noche oscura*.

In this sense, May sees that the 'dark night of the soul' can often be a much more mundane experience. We may not feel totally blind, but nor do we feel any sense of light either. We wander through an extended dusk. Driving to the shopping centre. Cleaning the bathroom. Heating a ready-meal. Again and again, going through the daily humdrum of life, with nothing happening at all, wondering where the hell God could be in all of this.

This has very much been my personal experience over the past few years. Vaux – a collective of artists, city-lovers and theological experimenters I was a part of for ten years or so – gave me a wonderful sense of belonging and achievement. We were living and breathing a cutting edge, emerging theology. Things were actually *happening*. And with its rightful demise a couple of years ago, I suddenly felt the loss of a lot of things that I believed gave me worth and significance. I was not a leader any more. I was not involved in any on-the-ground projects at all. I had young children, a demanding job and no time to even think about making video loops or creating liturgies, let alone curate services of other people's work too.

God, in many ways, became obscured, hidden. What I find profoundly helpful in May's work, as expressed by Rohr, is that it was precisely in this boring, ordinary, mundane time that God was doing hidden work. Why should God work in the dark? Because, Rohr says, if we could *see* what God were up to, we would either run a mile from it, or get our hands all over it and spoil it.

Paul's blindness after his experience on the Damascus road is a metaphor for God's sporadic blinding of us, but perhaps the silent years of Jesus' adolescence and early career as a carpenter, of which we know nothing, are equally informative. When our egos begin to take over, when we are in danger of hubris and when legalism and convention begins to set in, God suddenly becomes hidden. It is in these moments that we have a choice. Either we enter the desert and wait, trusting that out of it will come learning and maturing, or we continue to pedal harder, trying desperately to chase the night away.

As we face the questions, at our core must remain Volf's central question: *what kind of selves [do] we need to be in order to live in harmony with others*? When the darkness comes, who are we going to become? It will be tempting to try to keep the status quo, and to simply keep on what we have always been doing, 'dressing the wound as though it were not serious' as Jeremiah put it. This can take the form of trivialisation: we know that darkness is around, and that it is asking serious questions of us. So we pretend to enter it. We synthesise it, and simulate a sterile version of it, hoping that that will do. This is what we see in programmes such as *Big Brother* or *I'm A Celebrity Get Me Out of Here* – shallow heroes of our day being forced into faux-deserts to face heavily controlled 'challenges' that their agents have rigorously vetted. Nothing is learned here.

Alternatively, we may choose to try to outrun the darkness, worshipping harder and faster. Praying more fervently. Throwing our hands higher. Or we may simply switch on one of our many avatars, and play with them in some second life, in a virtual world where it is plasma-bright, without shadows. It is this choice that I believe is being taken too often.

So many churches have become afraid of the dark. Driven by success and the need to keep the money coming in to keep up the payments and keep the vibe positive, all mention of the night is avoided. But, as we will see, the artificial lights that are thrown up create strange effects. Desperate to avoid the painful mundanity of reality, they project a fantasy self, which ironically can only lead to darkness by another route.

x X x

The fantastic self: neophilia, cycles, spring

Thirty years before writing *The Seven Basic Plots*, Christopher Booker wrote *The Neophiliacs*. Its concern was to plot the 'fantasy cycle' that gripped English life in politics and the arts in the 1950s and 60s. With the Beatles, the Profumo affair and new directions in theatre this was a heady time in England, and in London in particular. What Booker did so skilfully was to identify the themes that connected so many of these apparently disparate events in different areas of public life. In particular, he saw that so much of history, personal and cultural, went in cycles, and in *The Neophiliacs* he aimed to sketch out the key elements of that cycle, drawing on the events of the day to show how it unfolded.

First comes the **Anticipation Stage**, where a real sense that something is about to happen is palpable. It is an exciting time, with everything seemingly coming together, pointing to the imminent birth of a new movement. No one is quite sure what form it might take, or the exact direction it may go in, but people are talking, conversations are happening, and desire is strong.

Then comes the **Dream Stage**, where the thing – the group, the ministry, the project – is begun, and everything is pure joy. Energy is high, and no matter what we turn our hand to, it all seems so easy and wonderful.

This is inevitably followed by the **Frustration Stage**, during which things are still going very well, but it takes a great deal more energy to achieve that 'high' than it ever did at the Dream Stage. This is when we see 'leaders' emerge as those who are prepared to drive the project forward by injecting energy where it is lacking, and trying to motivate people. This is in contrast to the Dream Stage, where the leaders simply need to channel the high levels of energy that are coursing around.

Next comes the **Nightmare Stage**, where it seems that no matter how much energy we put into something, the high is never achieved. Indeed, everything we seem to turn our hand to is hard work, or doesn't work. Relationships are strained and energy is very low. Leaders are feeling disappointed, and may blame people for letting the project down. It becomes hard to get people together, and when they do meet, conversations are difficult and strained. No one quite seems able to speak the truth about how they are feeling.

This is followed by the **Death-Wish Stage**, in which the project collapses and dies, with people within and around it all seeming to conspire to bring about its downfall. It may be painful, it may be cathartic. There is certainly a sense of relief among the leadership that they are finally 'free of it', and yet there can be longer-term problems with relationships that need healing. In death we are left bereft, awaiting a new dream, returned to the beginning of the cycle, wandering and wondering where the next scent of anticipation might come from.

I know now that I have seen this cycle repeated countless times in projects, ecclesiastic or educational, over the years.[45] Vaux went this way. Blogs invariably seem to go this way, as do political administrations. Indeed, I think everyone involved in leadership ought to be made deeply aware of this cycle before beginning any venture, since knowledge of the likely course of the project, emotional and spiritual, is going to be a huge help when the inevitable frustrations arise.

This 'fantasy cycle' appears to be completely unavoidable. Given that it is, that the reality of any project is that it will rise and collapse, why call it a fantasy? Booker uses the phrase not because the cycle itself is fantastical, but because we, as permanent fantasists, appear unable to see that each new thing we begin will suffer the same fate. We run around from project to project, church to church, job to job, always thinking 'this is *it*, I've finally found the real thing' – and are constantly surprised by disappointment.

Describing us thus, Booker coined the phrase 'neophiliacs' because he saw that those who seemed locked into this fantasy cycle were constantly in search of newness. Like those Jesus pointed out who ran around saying 'the kingdom is over here!' 'no, over here now!', we are a culture obsessed with the new, and quickly move on from one thing to the next, permanently believing the fantasy that *the next thing* will be the genuine article. The next thing will be permanent. The next relationship will never go sour. The next high will never wear off. The next church will be heaven.

It never is, and it is our ability to be conscious of this cycle working in all areas of our lives that forms part of the mature self that we are pursuing. We cannot expect to escape the fantasy cycle, but coming to terms with that fact is part of the process of being better able to ameliorate its effects, to make the booms and busts become more gentle oscillations.

We cannot expect to escape this cycle, but in Jesus we have the archetype of the person who did. In a wonderful twist to what is essentially a work of sociological history, Booker ends *The Neophiliacs* with a meditation on Jesus' time in the desert, and subsequent passion.

> In the wilderness, since he was a man, he was tempted, and to become a full man, had to wrestle with and overcome his fantasy self . . . In the events of Passion Week we see the

portrayal of the fantasy cycle, moving from the Dream Stage of the entry into Jerusalem with the crowds cheering, through the Frustration Stage of Gethsemane to the Nightmare Stage of the betrayal, the taunting and the trial with the same crowd which had cheered five days before, howling for his blood. And so to the Death Wish Stage of the Crucifixion.[46]

This would, of course, be the end of it – another failed mission from another would-be Messiah. But it wasn't.

On Easter morning comes the resurrection, completing the full cycle of the perfect man . . . The re-birth of Christ coincides, of course, with Spring – the rebirth of the year. But it is also a re-birth which can coincide with the inmost experience of every man [sic] who goes through the same pattern: of dying in his fantasy self, in order to live in his real self – the real self which, because it is part of God, goes on for ever and ever.[47]

Putting to death the hero, the martyr, the celebrity, within us means putting to death the fantasies we continue to hold on to. And this is what the night is for. Without the darkness, without the obscuring of God, we would persist in our great fantasies, believing the bilious fictions we act out, never having to face up to the truth about the imperfect groups we are part of, nor the damaged relationships that we involve ourselves in.

But God does not force us. When the night comes, when frustration arrives and God appears obscured, we have a choice. We can either blindly plough on, persisting with the fantasy that God is with us and all will be well, and thus drag people round as the cycle turns our close-held dreams to nightmare and death. Or we can wait quietly in the desert, speak nothing to Caesar, forgive as we are led to death, in the knowledge that, in the dark, in the moment when we are forsaken, when God is hidden, God is doing some work of maturity, putting another of our egotistical fantasy selves to death, and raising up our 'second life'.

This is then what loving the self will mean, this is the 'kind of self we need to be in order to live in harmony with others': a self that knows the dark, and sees that as the universal binding of all of us, and yet knows that another life lives beyond it.

Before we can move to take the speck from our brother's eye, we must come to terms with the planks that obscure our own vision. Like children, we are afraid of the dark. We turn to screens to keep our way permanently lit.

We know that we will not rid ourselves of fantasies completely. But we must also be careful never to let fantasies persist. The night will cycle round, and darkness will fall on us at some point, and we must be ready for the learning it will bring. We must enter the desert, all of us – all of our complex and legion selves – and face the darkness, the hunger pangs, the probing questions of the great Antagonist.

Time was when this should have been the rite of passage of every child as they matured into adulthood. That time has gone, but the journey must still be made, some time after the teenage years, preferably before the age of forty – the age of real leadership. We cannot tempt the darkness, or hurry it, for this is a work that is *done to us, not done by us*. But we must be willing to still tell stories of it to one another. Fictions, poems, myths, legends. The shared narratives of a thousand ancestors must continue to be spoken: if the hero is to live happily ever after, she must journey through darkness and become a worthy heir.

x X x

Conclusion: the differentiated self: separation, binding, centres

The fantasy self, the neophiliac constantly searching for newness, regenerating a new life by inserting another coin, never matures. The final tragedy of the online worlds we so often inhabit, the war games and final fantasy battles we participate in, is that – under most current gaming systems – these characters learn nothing. Enemies appear and must be killed, mutilated, ended. 'An enemy is a friend whose story you have not yet heard,' the saying goes. But this is not an option. Writing in the American literary magazine *The Believer*, Heather Chaplin summarises the problem well: 'Video games are good at fostering problem solving, but they're not so good at fostering human empathy or a deeper understanding of the human condition.' Comparing this with more traditional story forms, she continues: 'Novels are about psychological empathy; games simply are not. And if games are telepathing something about the future, maybe that tells us something about the future, maybe that tells us that psychological empathy, concern with the human condition is not going to be that important in the twenty-first century.'[48]

Somehow, we must make sure that empathy for the other and concern for the human condition are important in this undoubtedly digital future we are heading into. I believe that this is a work that must begin with loving ourselves – each and every self that makes up 'us'. We need to listen to them and sit down with them. Do battle with them. And, slowly, allow our true selves, the divine self within us, to become master. It is this true self that will 'become father and mother for others' – igniting the divine spark within them. It is to this simple task that each church, each community, each family, must turn themselves – to help others make this journey through the night and into the morning.

We have already seen how Jean-Paul Sartre reflected on our identity as being held within the paradox of facticity and transcendence, and how Allan Kaplan and others have encouraged us to become better aware of the processes that we are a part of, in order that we might escape the fetishisation of meditation, as Žižek puts it, and balance contemplation and action.

In *Exclusion and Embrace*, Miroslav Volf's wonderful meditation on 'identity, otherness and reconciliation', we are offered a further set of poles between which we can be energised. Volf examines how the Genesis poem of creation is marked by a rhythm of 'separating and binding'. Quoting American theologian Cornelius Plantinga, he writes:

> At first there is a formless void, everything in the universe is jumbled together. So God begins to do some creative separating: he separates light from darkness, day from night, water from land, the sea creatures from the land cruisers . . . At the same time, God binds things together: he binds humans to the rest of creation as stewards and caretakers of it, to himself as bearers of his image, and to each other.[49]

Volf explains how this creative activity of separating-and-binding creates patterns of interdependence. This process he terms 'differentiation', and goes on to claim that it is the separate-*and*-bound self, the interdependent differentiated self, that is the ideal.

Yet all of us dread both separation and binding. Babies scream with separation anxiety, not able to know whether the mother popping into the kitchen will ever come back, and this lower-cortex fear remains with us throughout life. At the other extreme, no animal likes to be cornered: we pace around relationships like lions round cages, wary of commitment, fearful of losing our freedom.

The differentiated self is the self able to divine the balanced path strung between these two poles. It is secure in its knowledge that it is separate, that, as an individual identity, it has a bounded space. Yet, at the same time, it is conscious of its interdependencies, that, in order to be fully human, it must be connected.

The fears that lie either side of this arête stem from the same concerns Bauman identified in *Liquid Life*: that of marking ourselves out as unique, while making sure people see that we are 'one of them'. They are the same fears that Sartre saw in those living in 'bad faith': collapsing the paradox of our identities into a list of easy-to-grasp facts, or withdrawing away from the other into transcendence.

Volf similarly sees the result of our fear of living in tension manifesting as a relaxation of the strain on one side or the other, i.e. an overemphasis on separation, or an overemphasis on binding. As he notes, 'exclusion can entail cutting of the bonds that connect, taking oneself out of the pattern of interdependence and placing oneself in a position of sovereign independence.'[50] We often see the self-sufficient, fiercely independent hero celebrated: the Dark Knight in the recent Batman films, Clint Eastwood in numerous Westerns. Yet this separated, cut-off figure is tragic. They have virtually no one to share their hidden identities with, and thus can never be 'complete'.

Similarly, 'exclusion can entail erasure of separation, not recognizing the other as someone who in his or her otherness belongs to the pattern of interdependence'.[51] In our desperation to include people, we can go too far and pay no attention to the boundaries that make us individuals. 'Everyone's special dear,' Elastigirl says to her super-fast son Dash in *The Incredibles*, refusing to let him run in school sports. 'That's just another way of saying no one is,' comes his damning reply. Refusal to acknowledge our individualities in a blind attempt to include everyone is simply another route to exclusion.

It is in this light that we begin to see Jesus' dawning realisation of himself as God and man as a model of the perfected self. In the desert, fresh from his baptism and affirmation by God, Jesus wrestles with who he is going to be, and we might interpret the first two temptations as pressures to emphasise his separate or bound self. By jumping from the temple he is clearly showing his supernatural power – his separateness from mere humanity around him. But by turning stone to bread, providing the poor with their basic daily food, he could be seen to be binding himself to the people around him, or at least making sure that they were bound to him.

In the end, he does neither. To have fallen either way would have been to bow the knee to his antagonist, but instead he sets out on a path that perfectly balances his separateness and binding. Miracles are performed, but friends are bound close.

It was vital that Jesus undertook a real journey towards his passion, the completion of the fantasy cycle. He could not have gone directly from desert to cross because the self has to emerge over time and in the course of interactions. Perfect in potential his self might have been, but perfect in practice it had to become. As Volf writes, 'the human self is not created through simple rejection of the other – through a binary logic of opposition and negation – but through a complex process of "taking in" and "keeping out".' Jesus, in other words, could not simply reject Satan in the desert, offer himself sacrificially, and claim victory.

In the same way, we will not be the mature selves we want to be by separation alone – as the ascetics would want; nor can we hone ourselves into maturity through binding alone – as social activists might think. Instead, we must consider our selves maturing through an ongoing, emerging process of differentiation. We must consider our selves maturing through the extended dialogue between the contemplative and the activist, between facticity and transcendence, between that which is separate within us, and that which is bound.

Simply because of the times we are in, I believe that it is in the context of our relationship to technology that this dialogue needs to be most carefully spoken. Just as in the creation story, the tools that we create, the technologies that we invent and evolve, are separate from us, and yet inextricably bound to us too. We need to accept the challenges of this apparent paradox, and not allow ourselves to be duped into accepting just one of the two positions. That will mean affirming that we are separate from our tools, that we can put them down. We will not die or lose out if we log off, or if our mobile goes dead for a while, or if we don't check our emails. It is towards this aim that Jews are right to keep the Sabbath: it is a day for putting our tools down, for affirming our separation from the machines.

However, we must not be fooled into thinking that Luddites are closer to God for their rejection of technology. Far from it. Whilst we might not die if we logged off for a few hours, for how

74

long would we actually survive if we gave up on advanced agriculture, modern medicine and heating technologies? If we are fit and healthy, we might think that we would fare quite well. But what about the old, the infirm, those who have suffered natural disasters? We tend to think of technology as electronics and digital systems, but these are simply one edge of a vast complex structure that we genuinely do rely on to sustain us, and in that sustenance there is a co-evolution between us and our machines. What is important is that we are aware of it, and are prepared to speak openly, truthfully, theologically and corporately about the effects it is having on who we are. There is no more potent symbol of the importance of this discussion than Jesus nailed to an instrument of execution, bound to a then-modern Roman technology, while in that binding simultaneously transcending all that it stood for.

In his later work, after the controversies that surrounded his views at the end of the Second World War, Martin Heidegger began to write increasingly about technology, often from the small hut that he kept in the mountains. His view was that technology is neither good nor bad, but that it is dangerous in the way that it becomes a prism through which we view the world as no more than a resource for our consumption. 'To a man with a hammer,' Mark Twain quipped, 'everything looks like a nail.' We pick up a saw, and can't see the trees for the forest of profitable lumber. Technologies, Heidegger was keen to point out, thus change the nature of the empathetic relationships we have with others. Unreflective tool-use will lead to violence to the other.

It is against this view of the world as no more than an enormous mall that Richard Sennett argues that we should return to the idea of being *craftsmen*: people who use tools in order to be engaged in good, thoughtful, careful work. Craftsmen (and Sennett explains that this usage is not ideal, but does include women) take up tools – use technologies – having reflected on the outcomes that they want to achieve *and* the manner in which they want to achieve them. Craftsmen are conscious of the ways that tools can positively transform the world for the good of the other;

75

they are aware of the empathetic network of relationships that encompass us, our technologies, our materials and other people. Upgrading to the latest model of plane every couple of months may mark a worker out as successful in that they can afford to do so, but it will have nothing to say about their abilities to work a plane carefully and thoughtfully, nothing about the way a well-used plane fits snugly into the hand and becomes a extension of the hand and mind that is sympathetic to the wood it works with. Jesus' early life and trade is not an irrelevancy; the fact that it is a carpenter who ends up roughly hammered to a butchered tree is part of the wider critique of our abuse of resources and technologies – and the violence to the other that results – that the crucifixion offers.

We begin to see then that somewhere between the separate poles of the true individuality of God – I AM – and the bound together mishmash of the crowds – 'I am because of everyone' – lies the God who became a craftsman and tool-user, humbly joined the crowds and yet refused their calls for celebrity. Jesus as fully God and fully human is our archetype, and we must journey as he did, engaging in the ongoing struggle to create the self. We will get it wrong – we always do – but we must continue to reflect and refine, putting down our machines and turning off our screens, returning to the desert for a while to reread our story, entering the clearing and letting the light play with the shadows.

'The self is never without a centre,' Volf says, 'it is always engaged in the production of its own centre.' If we are to become the kinds of selves that can live in harmony with others, then we need to be conscious of the centre that we are producing. We might glibly say 'we must be centred on God', but even as we do, we then hear Walter Brueggeman's warning that: 'we are indeed made in the image of some God. And perhaps we have no more important theological investigation than to discern in whose image we have been made.'[52]

As differentiated, complex, emerging selves it will not do for us simply to be told that we must be more Christ-like, for we now see Christ's life as an on-going theological investigation to discern in whose image he had been made. Being called by God, baptised and affirmed as God's child was only the beginning of the journey. It was a journey that took in deserts and high places, suffering and companionship, temptation and opportunity. It was a journey through dirt, towards the city, to face the other, to die and become the Father.

So if, as Christians, we are moving in the way of this Christ, we must accept the same path – complex, occasionally dark and difficult as it will be. But, like Jesus, it is a path that begins with affirmation: God *is* well pleased with us. We must allow this truth to be part of our reality. Simply accepting that we are accepted, loved sons and daughters maturing slowly into parenthood.

It is in the light of this love that our theological investigation must proceed. And so it is to God we must now turn.

Post-partum

Amniotics spilt, and semiotics rupture;
there are no words, just raw screams and suckles.
Child of God, child of man – no difference:
new life is unmoored emotion,
a wide sea of tears and sick,
and just one desire:
to feed, gather in, be mother-close.
But God won't stay.
Controlled crying;
separation an immediate fact post-partum:
we must learn to settle ourselves,
become content with occasional communion.

These all foretastes of a future rupture:
a larger curtain rent, another cry of pain
thrown down into Mother's hands,
three days to cry,
unknown seconds
before we may leave them.

PART TWO

LOVING THE OTHER WITHIN GOD

Embracing death and forgetting resurrection

The life that journeys slowly into parenthood is a life that also becomes increasingly aware of its own finitude. Children grow up and we realise that we grow old. Jesus' journey towards death fascinates us because we know that we are on the same path. As the only certainty at the end of each road we might choose to take it is no great surprise that philosophers, playwrights, musicians and poets have all found the mystery of death to hold a rich seam of creative inspiration.

The philosophers Emmanuel Levinas and Jacques Derrida have both reflected at length on death, not in a morbid sense, but with the view that it might be the ground of our ethics. The British theologian John Milbank summarises their perspective thus: 'Far from being complicit with evil as religious traditions have often taken it to be, [death] is the very circumstance that makes it possible to act ethically at all.'[1]

Levinas and Derrida argue that it is the fact that we *can* die that makes us vulnerable, and thus open to engagement with the other. Immortality, as Bill Murray comically showed in *Groundhog Day*, can be a depressingly invulnerable place and, as Milbank continues, 'it is the fact of death alone that lends serious gravity to the ethical demand which vulnerability imposes upon us'. In other words, given that I *could* give up my life for someone else, and that this act could not be a secret agent for my own power or earthly glory (because I am dead), then our readiness to die becomes not only the foundation of our self and of ethics, but also leads us towards an idea of God.

The reasoning goes something like this:

- It is possible for someone to give their life for someone else.
- If it is possible for someone to give their life for someone else, then it follows that it is possible that a vulnerable 'other' can place an ethical demand on us greater than our own lives, greater than ourselves.
- If it is possible that a vulnerable 'other' can place an ethical demand on us greater than ourselves then the 'other' must be greater than ourselves.
- This principle can be extrapolated universally so that the demand of the 'other' moves into the claim of the 'Other'.

This universal extrapolation is a valid move, Levinas explains, because death is something whose very existence is made of alterity, of otherness. It shows that 'we are in relation with something that is absolutely other' and thus death is that reality which confronts us with relation to an absolute Other.[2]

It is in the light of this thinking on dying for the other that we can then re-read Paul's words in Romans 6:6 that 'our old self was crucified with him so that the body of sin might be done away with'. Why is it important for us to die to self? Why should we take up crosses as Jesus did, and lose our lives in order that we might save them? Because it is in our vulnerability that we are drawn out of our selfish selves and into engagement with the other. Thus, ultimately it is the prospect of death – 'whose very existence is made of otherness' – that confronts us with the Other.

Nailing it

Modern/postmodern, epistemology
and philosophy,
arguments about text,
all distant hazes in the cortex
as this one true sensation
becomes all reality:
the pain of metal against bone
and blood and bitter wine;
hung in agonizing mezzanine:
Father above, who sent
and created earth below who received,
both now turning in rejection,
aiming at me their crude technologies.

Pig iron and sacrifice.
There is blood.
I am finished.

It is this 'Otherness' of God which confronts us in death that I think we have lost in much of modern Christianity, with the result that we have also lost touch with the 'others' around us. If we over-emphasise God as creator and sustainer, and, in particular, rush too quickly from the brutality and finality of death to Jesus' resurrection, then the power of death to engage us with the other is removed.

Jesus encourages us to take up our cross, but in doing so we need to walk as Jesus walked: not blithely confident in our own resurrection. Jesus feared death. He feared and mourned the pain and separation it would bring. In many ways resurrection is a gift that we would do well to forget about, in order that we might live lives that are orientated towards the other. Milbank outlines why Levinas (a Jew) holds this position: 'death in its unmitigated reality permits the ethical, while the notion of resurrection contaminates it with self-interest.'[3]

The finality of death presents it as a gift for which we gain nothing in exchange. Bringing resurrection into the equation changes the nature of this gift, and carries with it the danger that we might give our lives – knowing we will be resurrected – as an act of self-interest. Levinas is thus presenting death-without-resurrection as the ideal gift, or 'contentless' gift, where the giver receives nothing in return. If it were otherwise then the gift would be a selfish, rather than generous, act. However, this sort of gift is notoriously difficult, if not impossible to achieve. Even in death one can imagine that someone might be benefiting from my dying, and thus I could feel proud that my death has somehow become significant.

The danger here is that we can end up feeling that generosity is unattainable. The contentless gift is so difficult to give that not only can we not be generous in life, but even giving the greatest thing we have – our death – is infected by self-interest too. From the other side we have the same problem: those who have given themselves for us (those who have fallen in war, for example) deserve our unending thanks. This presents us with an impossible position: we feel indebted to humanity, and know we should sacrifice everything for it, but, as Milbank explains, we can't in any effective way:

> Where I cannot be reconciled with the lost one I have injured, I owe him an infinite debt of mourning and regret. So great a debt do I in fact owe, that my energies cannot legitimately be freed up to perform my duties towards the living. But those demands of the living also are infinite and infinitely legitimate, and so, here . . . arises an irresolvable problem: I should not cease mourning and apologizing, and yet I should.[4]

It is here that he sees the power of resurrection returning, because it is here, at the end of things, that there will be full and final reconciliation. He thus concludes: 'For the Christian, to give is itself to enter into reciprocity and the hope for infinite reciprocity. And to offer oneself, if necessary, unto sacrificial death is already to receive back one's body from beyond the grave. To give, to be good, is already to be resurrected.'

In bringing resurrection back for the dead Milbank asks us to go a little beyond Levinas. Our knowledge that death will come leads us to a common vulnerability and an engagement with the other – and the Other too. Yet it is faith in resurrection that prevents us from being obliterated by this huge obligation to serve the whole mass of needy humanity.

One very pressing issue regarding 'service to the whole mass of humanity' is that of climate change and our duty to the 'other' of the environment.[5] Thinking about reducing our carbon emissions and living more greenly is a classic example of the paradox that Milbank outlines above: we feel such an enormous and infinitely legitimate burden to save the planet – the Big Other of Gaia in James Lovelock's language – that we are paralysed and often do nothing.

Via television we witness the death of huge numbers of species and habitats, but feel powerless in the face of this destruction. Perhaps our conscience about the Big Other of our planet-wide ecosystem will only be moved to action when the smaller others of our family and community really begin to feel the heat of climatic events. Perhaps it will take a Hurricane Katrina in each country before we truly wake up to the way that our lifestyles are impacting people we don't know in ways we cannot fathom.

I feel that our faith has not always been helpful here. An unthinking belief in resurrection and renewal – the coming kingdom as a sort of divine *Groundhog Day* – can leave us not only believing that it doesn't really matter how we treat our planet, but even that speeding its destruction will bring God's intervention more quickly. Key thinkers like Alistair McIntosh and Dave Bookless have shown that this is both very poor theology and eschatology. Instead, we need a more balanced approach based on this resurrection paradox: the hope of resurrection prevents us from being obliterated by the impossible obligation that action on climate change demands, while our deliberate lack of presumption about it prevents us from lethargy that springs from a 'God will sort it out' theology.

In our theology as well as our ecology – and it is high time that the two came together in very significant ways – we have too often jumped too quickly to remembrance of our promised resurrection, and too little experienced the unknowing that Jesus must have had about death. In other words, it *is* self-interest that has contaminated much of our religion, and our eagerness to experience this resurrected God right here, right now, rather than reach out a hand to the other, is one of the manifestations of this self-interest. Just as we must learn to exist in the present with the paradox of our facticity and transcendence, we must also learn to think about our future in terms of a resurrection paradox: living with the hope of resurrection (that we might never give up and become swamped by the impossibility of the huge demands the needs of the world place on us) and yet never speaking presumptuously of it (lest we slip into laziness and inaction).

x X x

Embracing uncertainty and forgetting metaphor

I recently saw an example of the sort of message that comes with a collapse of this resurrection paradox on a poster outside an evangelical church down my road. 'Prayer', the text claimed over a graphic of a computer cable, 'is better than broadband.'

This is a claim to immediate communion with God that borders on self-delusion, and I have been tempted to knock on the pastor's door and ask exactly what he thinks this means. Admittedly, my Internet connection is sometimes rather slow, and does drop entirely from time to time. But, despite owning up to being an 'asymmetric' digital subscription service, it appears rather less asymmetric than God. Even on a good day, God's 'send' speed is somewhat slower than the typical believer's 'request' rate. Perhaps the divine server is under a constant denial-of-service attack.[6]

Even the most fervent evangelical Christian would have to concede the point: God *is* Other. God is not at the end of a telephone line. Prayers are not generally answered like search engine enquiries. Google is actually quicker.[7]

We are not yet resurrected, not yet at God's side, and to deny God's 'otherness', which I think the poster does, is futile. When pressed, as many have been in the past, and many continue to demand we are now, we cannot even prove God exists. So is theology then even sensible? In a world of hard science shouldn't we simply cut our losses and move from the centred self to how that self might serve others better?

Perhaps. But faith is not about what we are certain of. Indeed, the corollary of this – that faith means uncertainty – has been one of the tough lessons of the past few years that I have learned, and certainty about God is something I have had to let go. Having come from a place of certainty, or some mirage of it, I am with the agnostics, happy to accept that we will never prove that God either exists or does not exist. The scientific method simply cannot help here.

And yet when we look closely at science we find that it itself is possessed by some deep strangeness too. Those who reject belief in God as 'weird' need to make sure that they are ready to appreciate that the science that they defer to in place of 'wacky religion' has some fundamental oddities at its core. 'Those who are not shocked when they first come across quantum theory', Niels Bohr quipped to some of the best minds of the day at the Third Solvay Conference on particle physics in 1927, 'cannot possibly have understood it.'[8]

If its truths were bound to prove shocking to the intellectual elite in that audience, then the rest of us clearly have little hope of penetrating the mysteries of quantum theory. But, on reading Manjit Kumar's history of quantum theory recently, it struck me that the story behind the development of this new physics may offer helpful parallels for our situation with regard to belief in God, which also remains a shocking and strange position to so many.

Though Einstein was in many ways the father of the idea of quanta, he ended up rejecting the conclusions that the theory led Bohr to. Their disagreement centred on the fundamental nature of reality. For Bohr, quantum physics left him in no doubt that there was no such thing as objective reality. There was no 'real' world, simply a world that we perceived when we observed it. Einstein fundamentally disagreed, and argued right to the end of his life that there was a reality independent of our perception. This was not simply an obtuse argument about physics, this was about who we are and what the core of our life and existence is.

In 1926 Werner Heisenberg outlined his 'uncertainty principle', which requires that 'when the position of an atom is measured, the measurement process will leave the momentum of the atom changed by an uncertain amount inversely proportional to the accuracy of the measurement'.[9] Simply put: you can't at the same time completely accurately measure both the position and velocity of a particle. Why? Because in order to observe anything, our eyes, or some other recording instrument, need to respond to the photons of light bouncing off the thing we are observing. The problem that Heisenberg established was that at the sub-atomic level, a photon bouncing off a particle would actually cause that particle to change direction. In fact, this phenomenon is occurring all the time: every time we shine a light on something we are moving it ever so slightly, it's just that in the visible world of everyday objects the effects are totally negligible. But at the quantum level, these 'observer effects' are significant – and, without delving into the complex mechanical reasoning, lead to a basic level of uncertainty about a particle's state.

Physicists did not like what Heisenberg had to say, because of the suggestion when this theory is extrapolated that there is actually no objective reality at all – things only 'exist' when we actually look at them. It was this that Einstein objected to, this that led to major arguments with Bohr over many years.

Regardless of this division, one key implication of Heisenberg's work remains: as we attempt to look closer and closer into the structure of matter, matter itself becomes more and more elusive. In other words, though it may actually *objectively exist*, at some zoom level the world is no longer *fully observable*. The nice atomic models we hang in our laboratories, the graphics we see produced as people explain the CERN experiments – all of these are metaphors, all pictures trying to depict a reality that refuses to be drawn. Heisenberg's work demands that we abandon metaphors. At the scale we live and work in – metres, centimetres – there can be no physical models that accurately represent the world that exists at the sub-atomic scale. The only tool we have to probe deeper is mathematics.

I am not proposing to outline a mathematics of God, and nor do I believe that the unexplainable in quantum physics somehow is the new 'gap' in which God lives. But I do think that this uncertain, impenetrable, undecidable and unrepresentable side of scientific reality parallels well with theology and presents a principle that is humbling for all of us at a time when evangelicals and the new atheists are at one another's throats.

Multiverse (Perhaps I prefer the inefficiencies of this universe to the cold efficiency of your myriad others)

Relativity,
two clocks moving apart
at light speed never separate
and, in time, are forever together.

Yes, Albert,
as soon as you equalled the product
of m and c-squared,
you locked us in:
no information shall travel faster than light;
yes, our infinity, given a limit:
46.5 billion light years
to the edge
of us.

But you are there, and I here,
and strangely, from each centre elsewhere,
a new spacetime arcs out,
socking the eye with an infinite number of
observable universes.

And thus, inevitably,
an infinite number of you.

Some mother said I was unique, but now
a father's physics wants me to believe in
another me,
Beginning 10 to the 10

to the 29 metres far away.
Too far,
but somehow not far enough
For my comfort.

Quantum physicist,
Hugh Everett III, what have you done?
'The existence of other universes
is inevitable'
Said your Many Worlds Interpretation,
Which denied too the objective reality
Of wavefunction collapse.

And I'm like, WTF?

You go on:
'Between 0 and 1:
A single random number
With all its infinite decimals,
Is expressed, computationally,
Longer
Than
The computational expression
Of the whole set of numbers
That exist
there.'

Meaning?

Apparently this:
A universe of infinite parallels
May be more economic
Than a straight,
linear,
Singular
One.

Meaning?

Somewhere you and I are together,
Though, in this universe, we are apart,
And somewhere else there are more in betweens
Than we could ever fathom.
And that
may be more efficient
Than this.

And now my gourd is swirling,
Thinking,
What is love, and life and us,
Other than to trust in this membrane-thin world,
And chose to forego
The infinite possibility
Of the efficient multiverse,
And dig long
And deep
For life,
And love,
In this
One?

Embracing transcendence and forgetting immanence

Heisenberg's development of the uncertainty principle, and the whole discovery of the quantum properties of matter, precipitated a huge crisis in physics. Many great scientists of the day took a long time to come round to it, and preached vehemently against it – insisting that the progress they had made into the inner workings of the atom would continue and reveal a deterministic, objective model. They were proved wrong, and one by one, relented.[10]

For those of us who claim faith, there is a zoom level beyond which talk of God becomes impossible. This is the realm of faith. Our languages, our metaphors, simply break down in the face of some deeper, invisible reality. Though that reality may exist, we cannot observe it, and nor can it fully be put to the test. Are our theologies simply divine mathematics, full of complex symbols and attempts at integration? Perhaps no matter how complex their language or deep their thought, their imperfections, their incompleteness leaves them destined to be never quite true.

The uncomfortable realisation that the physical world was, at its core, 'strange' seems paralleled in the church by what we might call the 'crisis in divine immanence' over the past twenty years. As the crisis in physics gave birth to an iconoclastic movement of quantum theorists, reacting against what they perceived as the failings of classical theory, so the crisis of immanence in the Western church has perhaps precipitated the movement known as the emerging church – who in turn I see as reacting against the failings of what we might call 'classical theology'.

It seems no coincidence that the emerging church movement came straight out of the charismatic/evangelical wings of the church. With its hyper-immanent theology of Jesus being as good as touchable, it was the most obvious place for a group of young, enthusiastic but disaffected theorists to begin to doubt that there was an actual, material immanence at the core.

The model of church that these experimenters played around with was hallmarked by doubts about God's immanence. Services were dark and abstract. Songs, if there were any, were distant and vague, the soundtrack ambient, space-age, ethereal. Many groups began then to reject any talk of models at all. No metaphorical terms were useful any more. There was no body. Many have preached against it, and many conservatives and traditionalists have scoffed, like tweed-jacketed Oxford physicists, dismissing this emerging church as a fad that will pass. To their chagrin, it has not only refused to do so, but has become more and more part of the mainstream of Christian thought.

The arguments in the physics community rumbled on throughout the first half of the twentieth century. Neils Bohr and the young adherents to his 'Copenhagen Interpretation' continued to expound their thesis that objective reality was a myth, while Einstein, almost alone, stuck to his beliefs that time would prove otherwise. While no über-theory has yet settled the argument, time appears to be favouring Einstein: many physicists are increasingly willing to look deeper than quantum mechanics, and many philosophers of science now believe that there is an objective reality at the heart of matter, it's just that we don't have the ability to examine it.

I believe this is a useful position for us too: God is both real *and* unattainable. The evangelicals are right: there is an immanence to God, but God is actually not quite ready for the buddy-close relationship that they have marketed. The emerging theologians are right too: there is a strangeness to God, but objective reality does exist, so we should not be silenced by our fears that we cannot say anything about truth.

'God is light,' John wrote in 1 John 1:5, with perhaps more prescience than he knew: God, like matter, like light, is the perfect immanent-Other. It surrounds us, makes us, and yet will not succumb to full examination. It is an irresolvable duality, unquantifiable, immensurable and yet blindingly present.

We have seen the paradox of our own created selves in our separation from and binding to one another. Now we see the parallel mystery of the incarnation: God, through Jesus, is both separate *and* bound too. Just as the act of creation was a process of separation and binding, so the very creator, like the matter, the flesh, the blood, the sea, is separate from us, and yet intrinsically bound to us by his incarnation.

As the poster in my local evangelical, immanence-heavy church shows, we have been guilty of over-emphasising God's binding to us. We have claimed 'personal relationship', and sung songs like those with which we might serenade a girl at school. We have talked of direct lines of communication, of hearing what God wants us to do in the finest of detail. We have believed this God so bound to us that 'He' might put gold in our mouths, despite our fellow believers in the Sudan, or Ethiopia or Gaza, not even having bread to put in theirs.

In the midst of the recent financial turmoil I went to a large church and heard an exposition of the story of David and Goliath, which was aimed at encouraging the many members of the congregation who were involved in the financial industry. The message was clear: God is on your side and, though things may be tough, you will be protected.

I don't for one moment want to downplay the suffering some families will go through as they adjust from a very wealthy to a not-quite-so-wealthy lifestyle with the job losses in the banking sector. But this is the hard fact of the capitalist game we are playing: there are booms and crashes, *and God does not care*. Of course, God does care for our welfare, but I believe we are seriously mistaken if we try to bind God into preserving our wealthy and sumptuous lifestyles in the face of market forces within a system that we have bought into heart and soul. We are seriously mistaken if we try to bind God into preserving our carbon-rich

95

lifestyles in the face of an environmental crisis that our own actions have precipitated.

It is easy to love the God who is bound to us and answers our cries for help. But we are called to love the God who is other, who will not be bound to the destructive lifestyles that we pray are preserved.

If people need caring for, then the community of the church must act generously. But God will not be bound to our consumer-capitalism. God will not protect us from the financial downturns when we so joyfully reaped the rewards of the good times.

How have we ended up so convinced that God is so tightly bound to us? I believe that there are many deep-rooted problems that led us here, some of which concern a selective emphasis on 'binding' passages of God's care for people – the Exodus, the second part of Isaiah, the comforting Psalms – while simulta-neously skipping quickly over the many stories of God's wrath, God's rejection and judgement that pepper the Old Testament. We prefer to hear of God's everlasting love, rather than wonder at this totally free spirit who ups and leaves the temple, who allows his people to repeatedly fall into exile and suffering.

However, I want to explore two inter-related roots concerning what I would call the 'domestication' of God into a bound deity. The first of these concerns the birth narrative of the priesthood, for it is consistently the priests and leaders from time immemo-rial who have comforted the people with assurances that God is immanent, and will never leave them.

In Exodus 32, we see Moses tearing down the mountain, having just met God and worked out the Ten Commandments, to be faced with mayhem: Moses saw that the people were running wild and that Aaron had let them get out of control and so become a laughingstock to their enemies (32:25). Moses acts quickly and calls for anyone who is 'for the LORD' to come to him. The Levites – until then just another of the twelve tribes – do so. Moses' next command is extraordinary: 'Each man strap a sword to his side. Go back and forth through the camp from one end to the other, each killing his brother and friend and neighbour' (32:27). They obey, and we are told that around 3,000 were killed. A terrible slaughter, and yet their reward for this faithful killing was: 'You have been set apart to the LORD today, for you were against your own sons and brothers, and he has blessed you this day' (32:29).

I am not entirely familiar with the inner workings of the selection process for ordination in the various Christian denominations, but I'm fairly sure that a willingness to slaughter in the name of God is not an attribute that is tested very often. Let us not forget: the text clearly places the blame at Aaron's feet – he had let them get out of control. He is not only spared, but promoted to becoming the High Priest, the head of the Levites, the one through whom others shall meet God.

It is later on in Numbers 3:5–10 that we see how the Levites' role worked out:

> The LORD said to Moses, 'Bring the tribe of Levi and present them to Aaron the priest to assist him. They are to perform duties for him and for the whole community at the Tent of Meeting by doing the work of the tabernacle. They are to take care of all the furnishings of the Tent of Meeting, fulfilling the obligations of the Israelites by doing the work of the tabernacle. Give the Levites to Aaron and his sons; they are the Israelites who are to be given wholly to him. Appoint Aaron and his sons to serve as priests; anyone else who approaches the sanctuary must be put to death.'

It seems that the original priests, the Levites, were chosen because of their willingness to put to the sword those who disobeyed God. And this became their continuing duty: they were to camp round the tabernacle and kill any 'other' who approached, and were to be paid for this service by a tax 'levied' on the rest of the population. Their financial, spiritual and military obligations were thus intertwined.

The conflicts of interest are obvious: here is a clan of people whose sole task and source of income is concerned with protecting the place where God is said to dwell. Which of them would dare preach a message of God's absence, of God's otherness?

Which of us would dare? In this age of heavily professionalised ministry, with huge buildings to be paid for, and enormous salary rolls to sustain, who is going to preach any other message than that of God's immanence, of God's constant binding to us? In his critique of this mode of ministry, John Piper warns, 'Brothers, we are *not* professionals. We are outcasts! We are aliens and exiles in this world.'[11] Those of us in leadership need to be, like God, separate *and* bound to our people. To me this suggests financial independence at the very least.

The first root of our binding of God may then be rooted in our models and traditions of leadership. Yet the second root I want to explore concerns humanity's consistent vector of domestication in general.

In his Pulitzer Prize-winning book *Guns, Germs and Steel*, Jared Diamond explores one of the fundamental questions of human development: why some societies – like those in the West – ended up colonising other, far more ancient societies. Why did Spain conquer the Americas? Why didn't the Incas sail the Atlantic and conquer Spain? One only need read the details of battles that the Spanish conquistadors fought against the Incas to realise how pertinent the questions are to our theme.

On 15 November 1532, the Spanish explorer Pizarro met with the Incan Emperor Atahuallpa. Pizarro had with him around 160 soldiers. Atahuallpa was the undisputed monarch of the largest and most advanced state in the world, surrounded by 80,000 soldiers, all ready to die for their God-King. Believing they were on a mission from God – or the Holy Roman Emperor Charles I of Spain, if there was even a difference – Pizarro invited Atahuallpa to his camp, whereupon his priest, Friar Vicente de Valverde approached him and demanded that 'Atahuallpa subject himself to the law of our Lord Jesus Christ and to the service of His Majesty the King of Spain'. The text goes on:

> Advancing with a cross in one hand and the Bible in the other, and going among the Indian troops to the place where Atahuallpa was, the Friar thus addressed him: 'I am a Priest of God, and I teach Christians the things of God, and in like manner I come to teach you. What I teach is that which God says to us in this book.' Atahuallpa asked for the Book, and the Friar gave it to him closed. Atahuallpa did not know how to open the Book, and the Friar was extending his arm to do so, when Atahuallpa, in great anger, gave him a blow on the arm . . . Then he opened it himself, and, without any astonishment at the letters and paper he threw it away.[12]

Valverde was incensed by this apparent desecration of the Bible, and challenged Pizarro to defend God's honour. He did, and with just 160 soldiers, riding on horses and wielding guns, they murdered over 20,000 Incans before the sunset put a stop to the carnage. They then captured Atahuallpa, promised to free him, and murdered him too.

It seems extraordinary that Christianity came to this, that these actions came from those sincerely believing that they were following 'the law of our Lord Jesus Christ'. Yet, aside from the immorality of their actions, how did just 160 soldiers defeat such a huge army? Diamond concludes that the reason was simple: the Spanish had evolved into experts in domestication, and the Incas had not.

All humanity began as nomadic hunter-gatherers, foraging for food and water, never settling in one place. Then gradually, in certain areas, people began to domesticate wild plants and cultivate them into crops, and domesticate wild animals to help with this work. As agriculture developed, so people began to settle. Farming takes time, and requires people to remain in one place. It also requires careful storage of crops, and this led to the need for security – protection from other tribes – and thus the need for political systems and hierarchies, as well as division of labour as people worked on larger-scale irrigation projects. This in turn led to monarchies and empires – and, eventually, ships sailing to pillage and plunder other lands.

One of the many axes of history is the domination of the hunter-gatherers by those who had learnt to domesticate both crops and animals, and had begun to exploit the earth and its resources more intensively. This has been hugely positive: the rise of chiefdoms around 7,500 years ago meant that people began to learn how to encounter strangers without trying to kill them.[13] This in turn led to improved human rights and the rise of the social contract: the handing over of the right to use violence to the chiefs, in return for protection and prosperity under their rule.

However, it is important that we recognise that there have also been downsides. Domestication, as Diamond explores, appears strongly connected to violence and a religion of sacrifice. It is only through domestication of minerals that we have been able to make advanced tools, and thus cannons and guns and bombs – weapons that can kill our enemies without us ever having to look them in the eye.

Domestication of animals radically changed our relationship to our environment, and the price we paid was high. Diseases from livestock killed many (and with the rise of BSE and avian and swine flus, still do) and only those who developed immunity survived. We can thus see these survivors developing a morbid attachment to these creatures who sustained them with meat and milk and hides, yet had killed so many of their relatives.[14] The rise of a religion based on animal bloodshed and intricate food laws is then perhaps not surprising.

We are so used to living in a domesticated world that we forget that it could ever have been otherwise. It radically changed ideas of ownership and stewardship, and the power structures that rose out of it led, as we have seen in the story of the Levites, to a priest-based power-religion. In other words, it may be possible to plot a direct line from the domestication of creation to the domestication of the Creator.

We have house-trained God. We have localised, accommodated and claimed ownership of God, and fabricated a sort of divine social contract with 'him': only 'he' can use his great power to smite our enemies. We will be obedient subjects – so long as we are protected and prosper.

The bread and wine of the Eucharist are both symbols of this domestication. Wheat is a domesticated crop, grapes a domesticated fruit. Bread can only be made with heavy milling equipment, careful control of yeasts, and stable heat. Wine requires careful storage, and a great deal of time. Both represent the flesh and blood of a man killed as a sacrifice to an apparently blood-thirsty divinity who had made us lords over all creation – and both were part of a Passover meal that celebrated animal slaughter and divine violence.

In light of this I wonder if it might be possible to re-imagine the Eucharist as a meal of lament for our domestication of God. We pinned Jesus down in one place, and still cling to the efficacy of his blood sacrifice. But Christ would not be bound, and it is this free-spirited, nomadic God whom we find smashing a way out of the temple, out of the tomb, out of these man-made structures just days later, and encouraging his followers to eat in remembrance of this divine insurrection.

What would a 'Hunter-Gatherer Eucharist' look like? With wild grasses and spring water; 'freegan' foraged food and siphoned raindrops,[15] this would be a meal that celebrated our separate-yet-bound God's radical freedom, God's ungraspable objective reality singing beyond our impoverished metaphors, a God undomesticated, dirty and nomadic, free-spirited and unmediated by hierarchies and power structures, disinterested in blood. Moreover, the final challenge of this scavenged meal would be an affirmation that this God was not 'ours'.

God must be allowed God's freedom. Until we accept that God is not necessarily with us, that we may lose our jobs and our investments may go down as well as up, we will be worshipping a domesticated God. Binding God to our own agenda is convenient; it removes the possibility that God may, in fact, be more interested in the fate of the 'other' than in our own story. A bound God can only be a God of our own prosperity. This will not do. As Walter Brueggemann puts it: 'We will not have a politics of justice and compassion unless we have a religion of God's freedom.'[16]

Indeed, we will not have a peaceful society if we persist with domestication of God. Richard Wilkinson and Kate Pickett's argument in *The Spirit Level* is made very clearly: less equal societies always end up more violent. Thus, by binding God to our own agenda and setting up huge polarities of saved and damned, sacred and secular, in and out, we are creating, to use scientific language, big potential differences between ourselves and 'the other'. When fundamentalists preach fiery sermons about a violent God and emphasise our separation from the world they are actually putting more energy into inequality. This, Wilkinson and Pickett explain, can only lead to increased levels of violence. Why? Because increased inequality ups the stakes in the competition for status. Why is this important? Because with these increased stakes, the consequences of shame and humiliation – of loss of status – are also increased. As Harvard psychiatrist James Gilligan reflects, he has 'yet to see a serious act of violence that was not provoked by the experience of feeling shamed and humiliated and that did not represent the attempt to undo this loss of face.'[17]

Such questions of loss of face have a spiritual dimension too. By singing so hard of our longing to see God's face, we risk heightening the inequality between ourselves – with our presumed close access to God's blessings and riches – and the 'other' who, because they do not sing and seek as we do, is destined to spiritual poverty. This 'loss of face' of those who did not appear to be 'winning' the spiritual race was one of the major causes of tension in the church I attended during the 'Toronto Blessing' of the early 90s and gave rise to the same sort of feelings of shame, humiliation and loss of status. It wasn't so much a case of friction between those who accepted God was doing some very strange things, and those who didn't, but friction between those who appeared to easily access these odd places of intense communion with God, and those who wanted to but were left out. Why was God being mean to them? The smug glows on the laughing faces of those who rolled so easily in the Spirit did little to help, and many Christians I knew felt deep resentment and anger at what was going on.

x X x

Embracing immanence and forgetting transcendence

If evangelicals have domesticated and neutered God by over-emphasising 'his' binding to us, then equally others have denied God any power to act by over-emphasising God's separation. In the early days of the Vaux community that I was a part of, a minister came to see what we were doing. After the service he said that he thought it was great and exciting, but then asked, 'Where's the soup kitchen?' His point was a simple one: here was a bunch of committed, energetic young people with vision and time to do things. And here they were producing video loops and dark-glass graphical liturgies while, in the city surrounding them, people were going hungry.

At the time we countered this with what I believe are still good points: many of us actually spent our lives doing this stuff at work. We had people high up in the Youth Justice Board, another working for the Home Office on community development, another for an urban regeneration agency. I was teaching in a rough Inner London comprehensive school. In other words, we were doing things to help. But the minister's point continued to niggle, and I now think he had a valid critique: our exploration of the strange otherness of God left us highly sceptical of God's ability to work through us at all.

At the intellectual level, this had dangerous consequences too. I vividly remember talking to a friend about the nature of truth over a pint or two, and us wrestling with the question as to whether there was such a thing as objective truth. He vigorously denied it, and I asked a simple litmus-test question: was the holocaust evil? The logical conclusion of his then ultra-relativist position was that we simply couldn't say. My response was, if that was his view, I simply couldn't stay. We parted company in troubled mind, and I see now that one aspect of jettisoning any talk of God's binding, of God's immanence, is that we are left with a strange and cold God about whom we can say nothing, and from whom we can expect nothing.

x X x

Embracing a separate and bound Trinity

Jesus' command to love God, and love our neighbour as we love ourselves, is a command for a love that affirms both separation and binding. We have seen that love for the self means being a self that is bound to others, and yet remains essentially free. I look back now and see that the failed relationships I have had have all floundered on this point of balance: either I was too bound to the other person and thus suffocated their sense of freedom, or I didn't care enough for our binding, and demanded a freedom that felt insecure. As I work to become a better parent, metaphorically and otherwise, as I try to lead a life enlightened by the 'clearing' and tested by darkness, as I attempt to mature into the 'kind of self [I] need to be in order to live in harmony with others', it is to this task of balancing my relationship with this strangely familiar God that I must try to apply myself.

Once again, Fowler's 'Stages of Faith' model appears pertinent here. Stage 3, characterised by dependence on external authority structures ('the Bible teaches this', 'my pastor tells me this') and recognised most clearly in the evangelical wing of the church, would appear to default to an immanent/bound view of

God. As Sartre would doubtless never have put it, this is a view of God dominated by facticity, by a reasonable list of expected behaviours. At Stage 3 we are certain, our faith is strong, God is undoubtedly with us, and if we would only pray harder and be more holy (for Stage 3 is also characterised by the Protestant work ethic) then revival would come and God would be *here*.

The darkness of Stage 4, where authority structures are internalised, and external authorities doubted (most clearly recognised in the 'emerging' wing of the church) would appear to default to the strange/separate view of God. Again, as Sartre would not have put it, a view of God dominated by transcendence. At Stage 4 all is uncertainty, our faith is seriously under negotiation, and God is perhaps not objectively there at all.

Beyond these two stages, it is to the conjunctive perspective of Stage 5 that we should now be journeying. It is here that we are able to hold together different viewpoints simultaneously, here that we are able to accept God as both separate *and* bound, and life with God as something that does have an impact on the facts of our lives, while remaining aware of the 'abyss of personality' that makes both myself and God mysterious.

As we make this journey towards maturity, with all the twists and potholes in the road which that entails, it may be useful to consider that this is a journey that God has also made. The idea that God – the same yesterday, today and forever – has changed over history is a contentious one. (Whether it is God who has changed, or our perception and understanding of God that has changed over history is a moot point.) Regardless, if we look at the God of the early Old Testament – tempestuous, angry, violent, then graceful – it doesn't look a great deal like the same person we find in Jesus. The God of Genesis and Exodus keeps flip-flopping from total separation – casting people and cities aside – to unswerving binding, and this duality appears to continue throughout the Old Testament. On one page God is the victorious hero, ready to smite other nations for the Israelites, and then on another God is the aloof deity, unapproachable and unbendable.

We have seen that the true hero is not the one who wins the battle and lives in the eternal sunshine of the final-scene wedding, but the one who fulfils the true potential of that moment and becomes a parent to the next generation. The Self, Christopher Booker and others have shown us, is not complete until it has passed its DNA on.

It is in this light that we now see why the incarnation is so important: it was actually necessary for God to give birth to a son for God to complete Godself. This violent, moody, changeable God needed to grow up and become a Father before he could be counted as mature. As Žižek has argued, 'Christ had to emerge to reveal God not only to humanity, but to God himself.'[18]

God could not be all that God could be without becoming a parent. The doctrine of the Trinity is not simply about community with God; it is about maturity and growth *within* God too. The boyish, adolescent, tempestuous God of the Old Testament, of plagues and floods and animal blood, grows into adulthood and parenthood and, in one of those strange twists that Trinitarian thinking forces, allows the knives and anger of his youth to be turned on himself – not to affirm them, but to critique them and end them.

x X x

Embracing the stranger and forgetting the native

The God who flipped between extremes of immanence and separation now matures into the conjunctive Stage 5 of being both at the same time. In this sense we can begin to see God-incarnate-in-Jesus as the 'divine stranger'.

The stranger is a character who stands at the boundary of our knowledge. They are known to us because we have denominated them – even by giving them the name 'stranger' we have seen them and admitted their existence. But they are also unknown to us, or they would be called friend, or at least given a proper name.

Our relationship to this God who is both separate and bound, transcendent and immanent can be seen as a relationship with a stranger.

The sociologist Georg Simmel has reflected a great deal on what these un/known strangers might mean to us, and concluded that they play an important role in the development of societies. When they enter our world it is strangers who have to go through the painful process of adapting to our ways of life. In this way the stranger 'holds up a mirror to the society in which he or she enters, since [they] cannot take for granted ways of life that seem to natives just natural.'[19] The incarnation is God coming as stranger and holding up a mirror to our society. But, more than this, reading Žižek and Simmel together, Jesus' growth as a man who is finally forsaken – called 'stranger' – by God shows us Jesus holding up a mirror to Godself too. To God, Jesus became a strange man, but it was through this stranger that God learned about God.

The fact of Jesus' status as fully human and fully divine has traditionally been interpreted as a bridge between divinity and humanity: Jesus' divine side holds onto God, and human side holds on to us. But the idea of Jesus as the divine stranger suggests that the empathetic relationship may be equally powerful the other way round. The important thing for God was that Jesus was fully human – and thus gave God a strange mirror in which God could be revealed to Godself; the important thing for us was that Jesus was fully divine – for in this stranger, trying to adapt to the ways of our world, we see a truer picture of what we have become.

The stranger – the person who stands on the boundary of our community – is un/known. Because of the paradox of their nearness and otherness, the stranger is thus the one who teaches, the one from whom we learn best. Jesus was this perfect stranger. His temptations in the desert drew him towards performing stunts that would emphasise his otherness and miracles of abundant provision that would emphasise his binding. But, walking out of the desert to live among us, this stranger refused to collapse the paradox of separation and binding – to and from both us and God. In his death he experienced the agony of total separation; in his resurrection, the joy of full communion. In his temptations and pain he felt total empathetic binding with our humanity; in prayer and transfiguration, total separation from us. Now we, as Christians, need to seek to live by this same divine pattern: we are those who are both bound to and separated from God, and bound to and separated from humanity. Christianity then is not a religion of exclusivity, of a predestined group who are chosen for salvation. Instead it is the set of those who know/embrace this paradox of being strangers. We *are* the boundary, not the centre; we are the other, not the included, and it is out of this realisation that our empathy for the oppressed and marginalised springs.

As we think about how we might love the other within God we need to look for this hallmark: those who claim to love God will have a robust idea of God's freedom, of God's otherness and strangeness, combined with a keen sense of God's binding too. If I over-emphasise God's otherness, I will end up estranged and ineffectual. But if I over-emphasise God's binding, as I believe we have done in the face of an increasingly liquid world, then I know I am in danger of becoming a modern-day Pizarro, full of plundering and conquering, sanctifying violence in the face of difference. Jihadists and the Christian Right meet right here.

In the end, I know that this balancing act can only happen in community. My two eyes cannot discern the three dimensions of a life lived in proper perspective. I need others and others need me if I am, if we are together, to work out how this creative rhythm of separation and binding is to keep time. Similarly we know that if we are to love God and love our neighbours as we love ourselves, we must walk with our neighbour to discuss how we might better love our God and ourselves, and pray to God that we might more quickly become the kinds of selves who truly love the others, the strangers, who walk with us and around us.

x X x

Conclusion: embracing the dangerous place

The role of the priest, of the leader, has to be about creating environments within which celebrating and exploring this balancing act of God's separation and binding can occur. As we have seen, the birth-narrative of the Levitical priesthood is a troubled one, which appears to carry an idea of both protecting God's holiness from the people, and perpetuating the myth that God would never leave them. In contrast to this I believe that it is Jesus as the divine stranger who properly fulfils the priestly role.

In the Gospels we see Jesus drawing a community of friends and followers around him. There is healthy separation and binding, but Jesus never shies away from drawing them into what I would simultaneously call 'dangerous', 'dirty' and 'generous' places. They talk to strangers, and feed them. They talk to women, to Samaritans, touch those with leprosy, debate with Pharisees, dine with tax collectors. This is Jesus, supreme in his differentiated self, drawing his followers into a third place with strangers, so that both might experience transformation.

It is within this context of Jesus living and leading a community who are defined by strangeness that we might read his troubling words in Luke 14:26: 'If anyone comes to me and does not hate his father and mother, his wife and children, his brothers and sisters – yes, even his own life –he cannot be my disciple.'

These hard words come directly after Jesus has told a parable about a man throwing a great banquet. He invites those he is close to – but all reject his invitation, preferring to deal with their purchases instead. Angered by this, the host orders his servants to gather all the strangers, the outcasts, the marginalised and sick from the roads around the house and bring them to the feast. Is this not a damning critique of the lazy assumption of binding that the host's friends had? They assumed that there would be plenty of other opportunities. The host would continue to serve them when it suited. Jesus blows this assumption apart. Those who lazily assumed that God would remain bound to them, who got on with life's distractions comforted by the thought that they could turn up at the feast when it suited, suddenly find that the host has filled the house with strangers. The separate had become bound.

The parable is not simply a warning to those who assumed they would always be welcomed guests, but a guiding principle for those who would seek to be hosts: it is the strangers that you need to invite. It is among the strangers that you must prepare your feasts. Is this not what Jesus goes on to force home in his hard words about family? *If anyone comes to me and thinks that they can continue to assume undisturbed binding to their parents and family, they are mistaken . . . If anyone comes to me and does not expect to experience separation from their parents, separation from their family, they cannot be my disciple.*

Our journey into Christianity, into the way of Christ, has to be a journey into the way of identifying with the stranger. It is not a journey into refuge from the world, a journey into comfort. It is a tightrope walk between separation and binding.

Too often our churches are created as places of protection, exoskel-etal shells where we can take refuge from the traumas of the world and sing nice songs with like-minded, gentle people. This is not the church of Christ. Between our selves and 'others', church should be a strange third place, a place where the other and the self can meet and exchange gifts. It is the role of the priest, of the leader, to *facili-tate*, not dictate, these transformative spaces. It is our duty to learn to inhabit them for the simple reason that we are trying to follow a God who, through the incarnation, did the very same thing.

And thus we now see that, when Jesus talked of loving God and loving our neighbour as we love ourselves, he understood the inter-relation of these loves: the love for self that knows itself created separate and yet bound, the love for a God who has matured into a trinity, itself separate and bound, and now, as we turn to our final section, love for others from whom we experience separation, yet, in this journey of faith, find ourselves bound to in love as well.

Quarrying

Before plants, before animals, before fish;
after light, yes, but many days before you,
He called us up from the sea.
Hard, and strong,
we were the firstborn of all creation,
not you – soft, malleable, pliable, always yielding,
you who were created from our very dust.
We remained silent then.
You inhaled His breath, tried to forget your roots,
trod on us, though you knew our primacy.
We were your quarry;
you hunted us down, cut us and piled us up.
We were your weapons;
thrown in anger, from sweating palms,
boiling blood with merciless indignation.
But no more:
He came.
He came, and refused to turn us to bread.
He came, and said only the sinless could hurl us.
He came, and knew that if you, with your language and art
    and religion did not, then *we* would cry out.
Now we cry out:
You killed him.
The true cornerstone, the foundation came
and you ground him down
and trod him like dust,
back into the earth, forgetting your roots,
and cast him to us, rolled up

and sealed in an opening we had prepared.
For three days we kept our silence,
but then cried out: no!
We refused to hold him.
No soldiers had to heave that stone,
nor was it that the earth
could not hold him;
simply that it would not.
You buried the creator, and we pushed him back,
this God-man that gave us form and strength.
So speak now, you breath-filled creatures of dust.
Sing now of the miracle of your supple lives,
or we, the stones, will cry more
as you are lowered to us in your caskets,
and hold you tight and cold
until that day that you do.

PART THREE

LOVING THE OTHER WITHIN SOCIETY

Snow and strangers

In early February in 2009, the mid-afternoon sky darkened over London and a palpable sense of excitement rushed through the city: would it, wouldn't it?

It did, more than it had done for nearly twenty years. The clouds began to empty the cargo of snow that they had faithfully carried from the plains of Russia, and by the time Monday morning had broken it was clear: nobody was going to work or school. It was going to be a struggle to even leave the street. We listened in awe. A blessed silence had fallen with the snow: no cars, buses or aeroplanes to be heard.

Naturally, there was only one thing to be done. After a hot breakfast we all togged up in our warmest clothes, grabbed whatever slippery objects we could and kicked our way through the fresh drifts to the park. What we found there was a community at play. Angular teenagers, who would normally be skulking at bus stops and hiding under hoodies on street corners, were screaming with childish glee. Two skinheads were puffing their way up the hill pushing, inch by inch, the most enormous snowball, which soon became a five foot snowman. A young Spanish guy, living in London for a year and surviving on menial work, was generously calling for anyone to have a go with his snowboard – a thing he had bought on a whim and had little idea how to use himself. None of us had boarded before, but with numerous falls and shouts and lifts back onto our feet we worked it out together.

Snow in London is not particularly uncommon, but falls of this weight are very rare. Normally it is only a few hours before things turn to black slush, but this was here to stay. For two days the city was virtually at a standstill, with the news full of images of communities like mine doing what they so rarely do now: playing together. Of course, there were those who became grumpy about the whole thing, and spoke of the money that this would be costing the economy – one put it at £1.2 billion, an extraordinary figure that put a price of £200 per man, woman and infant on the head of each Londoner. Others moaned about the difficulties they had had struggling in to work, only to find that others hadn't bothered.

Seeing the snow fall so heavily I had had similar humbug thoughts myself; with the kids not at school on my day off I was going to lose my precious weekly writing time. Resisting the temptation to sulk, I ventured outside and began to see that I had been given a precious gift. Rather than sitting around theorising about the 'other', I got a chance to meet with and, most importantly, play with people from my local area whom I would simply never normally have had the chance to speak to.

This snow, these 'thin flakes like frost' from heaven, this icy manna, crystallised so much of what I want to say about engaging with and loving the other. It is simply this: our interactions with the stranger are so much better if played out on a different set of axes. Snow brings a strangeness to our landscape, and helps us to see its contours in a different light. Like the stranger that Simmel writes about, snow brings a renewed sense of the unknown to the known, and it is because we are thrown together as a community by it into this less familiar place that we find it so much easier to talk to those we would normally shy away from. The hard grid of economics, of work and profit and commuting, works against the possibility of meaningful engagement. This free gift of snow, unexpected and unsponsored, was the perfect bursting of the heavens into the everyday, and it is within these ruptured spaces that we so often find ourselves able to cross boundaries we had thought insurmountable.

What I am also now convinced of is the centrality of impermanence to the efficacy of these ruptures. Deep snow for a couple of days was wonderful. To have to deal with constant snow-drifts, sliding cars and icy pavements would soon create conditions in which I am sure that we would see a retreat further into our bounded comforts, and situations where friction within the community would rise.

The snow has melted now, though water continues to come from above in raindrops rather than crystals. Small changes in temperature and pressure; a radical phase change in a simple molecule; umbrellas, grim faces and traffic jams. The playtime is over for now, and I'm left hoping that I will remember some of the people I met. We were all scarf-wrapped, and never stopped long enough to exchange names. The simplex of that one-dimensional meeting didn't warrant it, but that simplicity lies latent now, the potential for complexity ready to arise – aren't you the guy with the snowboard? Didn't we exchange snowballs? Didn't you help push my car?

Christmas had long passed when the snow fell, but those few February days were picture-postcard scenes of winter and as we trudged through snowy woods near the house I was reminded of the carol:

> Good King Wenceslas looked out,
> On the feast of Stephen,
> When the snow lay round about
> Deep and crisp and even;
> Brightly shone the moon that night,
> Though the frost was cruel,
> When a poor man came in sight
> Gath'ring winter fuel.

The song is odd because it is only a part tale. We don't end up finding out what finally happened to the Good King, his page or the peasant they pursued with meat, wine and pine logs. The carol doesn't even go on long enough to say whether Wenceslas reached the peasant's home. We don't know whether he revealed his identity or simply left the gifts outside, nor if this mythic Good King did more for peasantry than this one generous act.

The carol is hagiography. Originally a reminder of the good life of Svatý Václav, Saint Wenceslaus I, Duke of Bohemia, who gave generously to the poor, it urges us to follow not just in his footsteps but in the warming steps of Christ who goes ahead of us when we help the needy.

I knocked on the door of a nearby family as we went out to play in the snow, wondering if their son wanted to come and play with my own. He didn't. He'd been out for a minute earlier, decided it was too cold, and was now inside playing a computer game.

Like the carol, we don't know ultimately where these journeys into the snow, outside the comforts of our warm castles, may take us and, given that this was the first proper snow anyone under the age of twenty would have known in London, I don't blame the boy for staying in the warm. But I wanted my son to realise this, at whatever level he could: to remain inside while it snows means missing out on something, being cut off from the generous little street-level exchanges that sustain life in the city. A shared snowboard, a helping hand from a stranger, familiar places covered in a new light. I didn't bother to make a rational case to him about it, but we did pull out a Christopher Robin book that night, and I read him A. A. Milne's *King John*, who, in contrast to the King Wenceslas of the carol, 'was not a good man':

> King John was not a good man,
> And no good friends had he.
> He stayed in every afternoon . . .
> But no one came to tea.
> And, round about December,
> The cards upon his shelf
> Which wished him lots of Christmas cheer,
> And fortune in the coming year,
> Were never from his near and dear,
> But only from himself. . . .

> King John stood by the window,
> And frowned to see below
> The happy bands of boys and girls
> All playing in the snow.[1]

Like all of us of course, even this bad King John 'had his hopes and fears'. We have been on a path of increasing individualism for so long that we too may frown to see people at play. Like King John, we must pray for rupture, and be prepared to catch it when it comes:

> A while he stood there watching,
> And envying them all . . .
> When through the window big and red
> There hurtled by his royal head,
> And bounced and fell upon the bed,
> An india-rubber ball!

As with the carol, Milne leaves us to imagine what happened once the rupture came, but I like to think that perhaps he took that fine rubber ball down into the street, called some of the children over and began a game.

Part of the power of Milne's poem about King John lies in its sense of elevation. It begins on the ground with him 'walking in the town', but being snubbed by the townsfolk and leaving him 'blushing beneath his crown'. From there on in King John remains inside his castle, having tea on his own and rising further above the streets that hurt him to the top of the chimney on his roof, wherefrom he appeals to Father Christmas for help. As it turns out, the gift eventually comes from the street below – a ball thrown in through his window. King John, despite his wealth and power and elevated status, is lonely. He simply wants someone to share his life with, but, as Wilkinson and Pickett show us in *The Spirit Level*, the vast income inequality that sets him as king far above those in the street below leaves him isolated and fearful, frowning at the teenagers playing out in the street.

x X x

Loving and living

It would be too grand to read much divinity into a ditty written for a six-year-old, but there is a sense in which this view of the aloof monarchy persists in the popular view of God. Snubbed and offended as he walked with us, God has retreated to heaven and now looks down on us like a feeble tyrant; we carry on regardless, 'giving him a supercilious stare, or pass[ing] with noses in the air' while God 'stands dumbly there', powerless and miserable.

For 'God' or 'King John', we might easily read 'the church'; for 'the church' you might easily read 'me'. As Henri Nouwen has so honestly put it 'I am so afraid of being disliked, blamed, put aside, passed-over, ignored, persecuted, and killed, that I am constantly developing strategies to defend myself and thereby assure myself of the love I think I need and deserve.'[2] At the slightest rebuke we raise our defences, retreat into our castle-like churches and serve tea while no one comes. Just as we do this corporately, I am aware that I do it personally too, pulling up the drawbridge of my self, battening myself down with books and headphones. In doing so, Nouwen carries on, 'I move far away from my father's home and choose to dwell in a "distant country" '.[3]

The interplay of metaphor here is informative. King John's response to being wounded was to isolate himself in his castle – with its tea for one and empty rooms it has lost any sense of being 'home' – and Nouwen describes the Prodigal Son's parallel action: to leave home entirely, to leave his community and people behind and disappear into the anonymous crowds of a foreign place. Locking our selves away or disappearing to another place entirely: both are critical rejections of the 'others' who populate the streets outside our doors; both are strategies we employ to protect ourselves from having to engage the other, from having to deal with those around us who are connected to us.

We see both strategies projected onto our views of God: the miserable Father in heaven, locked away and accusatory, or the unknowable non-entity, so far away as to be disregarded.

We can see both strategies in the church: buildings and services fortified against welcome, missions boards thumb-tacked with photos of those we support in far off places. We don't fear reaching out to those who in turn are out of reach. We can support African children precisely because they are in Africa; the issue of disaffected children on our own streets is far more problematic because it may require us to do more than put our hands in our pockets. We might actually have to get our hands dirty.

The irony of this sterilised view of mission is that our faith is based on the fact that things did get dirty. God becoming human is God getting down and dirty with all that humanity entailed. And, using Mary Douglas' definition of dirt as 'matter out of place', in Jesus' passion we see the most filthy sight ever: God cursed and hung on a tree.

One way of reading the incarnation is simply this: in it we see God simultaneously refusing to be taken for a miserable crank and refusing to disappear and be forgotten. These are the two paths that the Old Testament offered – God locked away unapproachable in the Holy of Holies, and then God removing himself from engagement with sinful Israel, as we see in Ezekiel 10 with the departure of God's glory from the temple and the scattering of Israel far and wide in the exile.

God, separate from us yet bound by love to us, rejects both of these paths. Holiness and separation had proven useless in transforming either God's anger or our behaviour. With the incarnation we see the core message of Christianity built around a new, dirtier principle: to *love* the other, we have to *live* the other.

x X x

Unblocking and adjusting

The only natural response of God's love was carnal: to enter into a body and get to grips with what humanity was facing. Using Allan

Kaplan's language, the incarnation can be seen as the ultimate act of 'social process': this was radical, divine, development praxis. The old prophets and the tablets of the law were like arms-length aid packages dropped from on high from military supply planes. *Here's how to be better, now get on with it and don't say I didn't help you.* What Kaplan is arguing in *Development Practitioners and Social Process* is what all development professionals know deep down: it's only through intimate involvement with local processes that aid makes any long-term difference.

The risk of the food-parcel aid culture is that we create a people totally dependent on hand-outs. Is this not what we are in danger of creating in the church? Don't we risk producing generations of Christians unable to think or act or create for themselves because we've made them totally dependent on the rations thrown out of aeroplanes by the latest big conference shticks?

It is against this sort of supply-plane intervention that God in Jesus creeps into our world, virtually unseen. For nearly thirty years he says nothing of note and does very little to make himself noticed. Instead he listens, watches, reflects and ponders the question of what it is to be human, and what it is in our human condition that has separated us from God.

At the beginning of his ministry, as we have seen, he is tempted to take the spectacular approach to development: to throw bread at hungry people, to perform incredible stunts and stun them into changing their ways. But he resists. Softly, gently he begins to tell stories, planting seeds of change and moving on, going so far as to die and disappear even before any fruit of this labour was secured.

We re-read Kaplan's words in this new light: 'as social practitioners – whether consultant, leader or constructive participant – we are there to work with the organism's process. As such, we have to learn to read and recognise the underlying patterns, and help unblock or adjust, so that the ongoing process of development may unfold once more.'[4] This is a superb summary of Jesus' ministry. He came to work with our processes. He came and became in order to learn to read and recognise the underlying patterns of our behaviour, and worked a miracle of unblocking so that we might be free to develop once more – free, rather than forever dependent.

This is what true love does. This is what true hospitality does. It doesn't create dependency, but freedom. Any relationship that leads to addiction, to codependency rather than interdependency, is a distortion of this love. Any involvement that leads to victims becoming forever dependent on donors is inadequate social process and is certainly not *development* in the healthy sense. This is true at whichever zoom level we care to look: love, whether for self, God or neighbour, is about a commitment to understanding the processes and cycles of a person or community so that any flows might become 'unblocked'.

So as we come to look at what it might mean to love our neighbour, to love not just those neighbours who are lovely, but those who are strange and other, I want to propose two core values that might guide our interactions.

First, we should lean towards locating what we do in the economy of gift, because it is only here that what we do can truly be about the other, rather than our own profit. It is only within the spirit of true generosity that we can begin to remove the ego from our work with the other, and thus attempt to do things that are marvellous, rather than spectacular. The gifts of shared music and shared food are two ways that I propose we might do this.

Second, we should lean towards the temporary, because it is only in the temporary that the violence that is required to sustain permanent utopian structures is mitigated, and only in the temporary that new axes can be inhabited, within which we again become stranger in order to better empathise with the other. As I shall explain in depth later, it is within the context of temporality that we can move away from being strategists – those who plan and scheme in order to take the reins of power – to become insurrectionists and tacticians – who have no interest in power. Similarly, we shall see that it is within this spirit of generous temporality that we will move from being tourists to pilgrims, and reinvigorate our faith with the orthodox heresy of piracy.

Permeating these two core values will be the key principle of the incarnation: in order to minister to us, God had to become the divine stranger among us, listening and striving to understand our cycles and processes and becoming fully engaged in them. This was an inherently dirty process, full of challenges and ruptures. True love is never sterile fetish or fantasy. True love is involved; true love pursues, even into the darkest, dirtiest places. What we will find there is the face of the other, and it is in the held gaze of that face that we will realise our interdependence: the fate of our lives and beyond are tied up together.

Vectors

Down?
Is this your vector?
To earth, from heaven, and further,
Beyond into hell.

Or up?
Is this your vector?
Bread lifted, body raised, and further
than I or any could tell.

Or among?
Caring not for vectors.
infecting, uniting, and further
disturbing this earth where we dwell.

x X x
Gift

Key to the smooth flow within and among the cycles of love for self, God and other is the idea of balance. Balance and compromise are two responses to situations of tension. Compromise is designed to remove the pressure between two opposing positions; compromise is what politicians do when faced with conflicting lobbies over an issue. They try to diffuse tension and to draw ideas from both sides so that both feel they can own the solution. Compromise is political expediency, and sometimes compromise is very important. However, compromise can lead to stagnancy, to a feeling that neither side has made any progress. Compromise can feel far removed from the 'unblocking' that Kaplan aspires to.

As an alternative he proposes the idea of balance. When there are multiple tensions pulling on an organisation, an attitude of balance seeks to exploit the energy of both positions so that they move the body forward, rather than rip it apart.

God's immanence and otherness are not a compromise. God as separate and bound shows a divinity in perfect balance, and it is out of this balance that the energy comes. As we have seen, God fully immanent and God fully other are both zero-energy positions. It is only in the dialectic, in the opposition of these two states, that energy is created.

We can see this same energetic tension within ourselves: we are strange, and yet we are close. There are battles within each of us that are exciting and important. We see it again in our relationship to the tools we create and which inevitably recreate us. We must use the energy that comes from a balanced approach to new technologies, rather than collapse into the tensionless positions of unquestioning adoption or flat rejection.

So as we consider how we might engage the other, we need to affirm that we will not be looking for compromise and nor will we be able to eliminate tension. Instead, we will be looking for balance, for the energetic state where the processes that make up ourselves, and those around us, are evolving dynamically.

If this sounds like an ethereal goal to attain, then it is worth affirming that that is exactly what it is. Beyond the physical exchange of resources, beyond the giving of humanitarian aid or the dispensing of medicines, beyond the hospitable donation of food to the stranger, is the intangible place of gift. Anyone can throw food from the back of a lorry to hungry people. What takes the donation from the realm of industrial food distribution to that of hospitality is the incommunicable spirit within which it is done, the ache that longs to get to the root and make sure that this never has to be done again.

It is for this reason that Kaplan has called those attempting to follow the new models of development and social process as 'artists of the invisible', and this, I want to argue, is what faith communities need to be aiming at when engaging the other: an approach that is informed by artistry.

Hamburgers and gifts

Mission involving food distribution is a good case in point. Food – whether being bought in supermarkets, distributed by aid agencies or hunted in forests – is a powerful signifier of our attitudes and beliefs. What we eat, and how we relate to food in general, says a great deal about who we are.

I know of a church which set up a burger van in a town centre as a way of attracting new people. The idea was simple: they would give away free burgers as a way of beginning to engage people in evangelistic conversations. That the food they were offering was unhealthy, of poor quality and from questionable animal husbandry, coupled with the fact that they angered those in the town centre square trying to make a legitimate living from vans selling food, clearly showed that they had not thought out the various gift and commodity exchanges that their ministry entailed.

In one sense their thinking was correct: when we share the gift of food new spaces are created where other gifts can be given and received. We invite people for dinner and our relationships with them are enriched and deepened. But when we exchange gifts of food we need to be aware of the other cargo that can come with it, and in particular the way that gift exchange can be a way of exercising power.

Aside from the issues mentioned above, one of the reasons I think this church was wrong to use burgers in this way was that it was a gift that was heavily loaded with other cargo. First, because of the latent power of gifts of food, people receiving a free meal do feel a pressure to give something back in return – in this case some time to 'have a chat' with someone from a church. Second, the reception a gift like this will get can be difficult to predict. For those who are hungry and unable to buy food – a position none of the people in this quite well-off town in the south of England would have been in – the gift of food is a lifesaver. But the very act of accepting a charitable donation of food is a tacit acceptance of one's position as poor and needy. It can therefore lead to feelings of humiliation. For those who are not starving but are still poor, like some of the people in that town, the perception that the donor may be thinking you are in need of charity can be equally humiliating.

A good example of this is seen in the classic children's book and film *The Railway Children*. Three wealthy English children and their mother end up fleeing to a cottage by a railway in a northern village as their father is wrongly sent to prison for spying. Having befriended the stationmaster at their local stop, they find out it is his birthday and set out to collect donations of presents from everyone in the village. Some give food, others useful things for the house, another a pram for the baby. Presenting all this at a surprise party for the stationmaster, they are shocked to find him utterly humiliated by the gifts. The cargo that he perceives comes with them is that the entire village must think him unable to support his family and in need of charity. It is only after he has become enraged and thrown the children out that they beg to explain that in fact the gifts were all given in love – the people of the village adore him. Thus restored, he allows himself to accept the presents and is very thankful.

As the stationmaster was too keenly aware, gift exchanges can very often be about displays of power, and Jesus understood this perfectly. In Luke 7 he is dining with a group of Pharisees who become embarrassed when a 'sinful woman' comes into the room and washes Jesus' feet with her tears, an expensive jar of perfume and her hair.[5] The story is slightly problematic in that we read that the 'Pharisee who had invited [Jesus] saw this and said to himself . . .' and of course we have no way of knowing how Jesus heard what he'd said under his own breath. Even so, the dramatic intention is clear: 'I came into your house,' Jesus says to him. 'You did not give me any water for my feet, but she wet my feet with her tears and wiped them with her hair. You did not give me a kiss, but this woman, from the time I entered, has not stopped kissing my feet . . .'

What is important to note from this story, and others like it in the Gospels, is that Jesus understands that *all* gifts, even the absence of gifts in contexts where it would have been customary to expect them, carry cargo. That the Pharisee had not offered the customary foot wash or kissed greeting to Jesus when he entered his house is a powerful statement of his disregard for Jesus. Equally, the woman's flamboyant offering is a powerful statement of her high regard for him. Both gifts say something about the perceived power-relations between the giver and receiver. The Pharisee wanted to be seen to be entertaining Jesus, so invited him to share food – yet his neglecting to offer the simple things of hospitality on Jesus' arrival betrays his real motive. His gift of a meal to Jesus was loaded with cargo: I am wealthier than you and more important than you; I can afford to give food to a poor itinerant preacher, but I won't pretend to really care about you.

The woman, on the other hand, clearly felt hugely indebted to Jesus, perhaps for his respectful treatment of her. Her tears are a gift welling up from within. Her hair, which in her line of work would have been integral to her need to be alluring, is sacrificed as a towel to dry a foot, and perfume which she could perhaps barely afford is poured out liberally. These gifts came loaded too, but their cargo speaks of poverty of spirit, rather than pride. Her sacrifice is genuine, for the passage tells us it comes from her love for another; the Pharisee's 'sacrifice' is rejected, like Cain's offering, because its voice sings only about himself.

Given that both gifts came with other cargo it is perhaps worth considering if, outside of the immediate context, Jesus would have been critical of both the Pharisee and the woman. We read at the beginning of Matthew 6:

> Be careful not to do your 'acts of righteousness' before men, to be seen by them. If you do, you will have no reward from your Father in heaven. So when you give to the needy, do not announce it with trumpets, as the hypocrites do in the synagogues and on the streets, to be honoured by men. I tell you the truth, they have received their reward in full. But when you give to the needy, do not let your left hand know what your right hand is doing, so that your giving may be in secret. Then your Father, who sees what is done in secret, will reward you.

Neither the Pharisee nor the woman did their giving in secret that night. One gave in the right spirit, yes, but both were very public displays of generosity. Is Jesus contradicting himself by not chastising the woman for following his teaching? If it would have been ungracious to point out the lack of secrecy in her giving, was it not also insensitive to embarrass the Pharisee in his own home?

As with so much of the rest of the Sermon on the Mount, Jesus is giving us a goal to aim at, knowing that we will probably fall short in practice. He is visionary, and yet pragmatic: each hand will always have some idea what the other is up to. This mixture of graciousness, realism and intelligence is important if we are ever to remain generous in our giving and receiving. To analyse each gift too carefully is to risk hardening your heart to the generous spirit, however clouded, that is offering something to us; to accept every offering without consideration of the cargo that is coming with it is to naively open oneself to manipulation.

The philosopher Jacques Derrida spent a great deal of time puzzling over the problems of gift, and whether it was even possible to give a truly pure gift that carried with it no cargo. As we have seen previously, this problem of the 'contentless gift' had taxed Levinas too, and much of Derrida's work is a response to his thoughts. Both of them saw that the ideal gift was one where the giver received nothing in return, because this showed that the gift was purely sacrificial, carrying no element of self-interest. But this proves to be an impossible task because, to use Jesus' example, even if the right hand does not know what the left is doing, the brain can carry a sense of pride and self-satisfaction from being generous, even if the giving is done in secret. If I give a gift to someone without putting my name on it, I still receive a feeling of well-being in return which sullies the purity of the offering. Analysing the problem ever more deeply, Derrida concludes that the only genuine gift must 'involve neither an apprehension of a good deed done, nor the recognition by the other party that they have received'.[6] In other words, the receiver doesn't know that anything has been given, nothing actually *is* given, and the giver doesn't know that they have given either. He then goes on to show that this could only occur in a situation where the giver and receiver, the self and other, were 'radically disparate, and have no obligations or claims upon each other of any kind'.[7] It would seem then that the only way we can be truly generous is to withdraw completely from the other – a position that Derrida knows is nonsensical.

In his book *How (Not) to Speak of God*, Peter Rollins has argued that forgiveness, done silently, could be one way to approach a more ideal gift that does not reduce relationships to an absurdity of coldness and distance. First, one can only consider forgiveness to one to whom one has some kind of connection. Second, nothing is physically given, and the receiver may have no idea that they have been forgiven. Third, the problem of feeling good about oneself still remains, but true forgiveness is no matter for pride, and so this ought to be reduced. Beyond that though, Rollins then explores how it is love that stands behind and beyond this as the true manifestation of generosity:

> Is this not what the biblical injunction, to give so as the right hand does not know what the left has given, really means? The love that arises from God is a love that loves anonymously, a love that acts without such self-centred reflections, that gives without thought. Our lives should be full of acts of love of this kind and yet, by definition, they will be invisible to us.[8]

The root of Derrida's double bind is the problem of selfishness within giving, which he attempts to unravel by extending the distance between the self and other to infinity and the size of the gift to the infinitesimal. But now a new way opens to us: the perfect gift may be out of reach, but we can approach it not by removing ourselves from the other, but by removing the self – the ego – from the transaction. This is the paradox that Rollins expresses well: our journey to become 'the kind of selves we need to be in order to live in harmony with others' is both a journey of becoming more aware of the self, of seeing clearly who we really are, and simultaneously a journey of dethroning that egotistical self in favour of love. As Rollins writes, 'we must let go of ourselves in such a manner that we can become a dwelling place in which God can reside and from which God can flow.' Why should we attempt this? Because, as he continues, 'The hope is that in so doing love will flow from us.'

We will, in other words, begin to love the other when we love ourselves enough to allow God – who is love – to lead us. This is God's lesson of the incarnation. It was not enough to walk with us in the garden and give us this loaded gift of creation and freedom. It was not enough for us and God to be 'radically disparate, and have no obligations or claims upon each other of any kind'. The only way that we could be transformed, the only way that we could be prepared for this mysterious and invisible gift of the Spirit, was if God dethroned himself, dressed himself in our own skin and, in love, became a dwelling place from which God could flow. This was the body of Christ. This is the embodiment to which we are called.

Redemption song

Oh you quavers and crochets,
minims and breves,
step down from your clefs
and forget your times:
the strict beating of the 4/4,
the 3/4, the 6 over 8
and sometime 7,

gather here with rests,
and stop.

The composer waits,
pen over paper,
a dance in ink yet to begin
in the mind and
shiver down the spine
to fingers clutching quill.

The notes gather and listen,
waiting to be born in rhythm,
to flow under rhyme and
skip with reason.

The sounds hold back,
ready to pour forth their waves
in full crescendo at his command:
'Let there be music'
and the song begins.

The beat will drive
and stamp its foot:
No. No. No.
The melody will persist
while the harmony rejoices
in hope and
the lyric speaks out,
this shattering song
of coming redemption.

The conductor stands.
The audience hushes.
A breath is taken,
a foot shuffles.

The baton strokes the ending silence:
one, two, three, four . . .

Music and feasting

If we are to become 'artists of the invisible' we must appreciate that the true gift that we give – beyond the food, clothing and shelter – is invisible and, moreover, that we ourselves should be trying to be as invisible as possible in the offering too. We have seen forgiveness offered as an example of a more ideal gift, but I would like to add music and feasting to that list too.

Claude Levi-Strauss wrote in the introduction to *The Raw and the Cooked* that music is 'the only language with the contradictory attributes of being at once intelligible and untranslatable . . . [it is] the supreme mystery of the science of man'.[9] It is also a gift that is often best received blind – disconnected from those making it.

Some years ago I went to see the Icelandic band Sigur Ros play in London. The gig was for the most part good, but ended in quite extraordinary fashion as they played the achingly beautiful final track from their un-named third album. A curtain was drawn across the whole stage and lights were projected on to it from behind, leaving the band invisible. Singing in what was basically an ecstatic tongue and playing behind a veil, the music was elevated to a place untarnished by a singer's ego or a guitarist's posturing.

Given direct access to the pre-language parts of our brains, music is able to lift us out of the particular and into the mysterious universal while remaining but a *vehicle* to this place, rather than being something tangible we receive itself. Thinking back to Roger Scruton's description of the sacred as 'moments that stand outside time, in which the loneliness and anxiety of the human individual is confronted and overcome, through immersion in the group', we can see how good live music is essentially a sacred space. It is unfortunately a space too often tarnished with ego and celebrity.

It is my hunch that one of the key ways in which we should work to engage the other is through this gift of shared music.

Unfortunately, too much church music – whether in choirs or attention-grabbing worship leaders – lacks this invisible quality. Too often music in church is castrated and forced, eunuch-like, to serve one bland and narrow purpose: to lead us from one section of a service to another. Too infrequently do we find mystery, beauty or ecstasy; too infrequently is our auditory cortex zapped, sending crackles of synapses pulsing into raw emotion.

More importantly though, too frequently do we find music employed in advertisements and services to whip up emotions, and too infrequently do we find music simply being enjoyed and shared. Songs are the musical story of us: our culture, our history, our loves and losses. To share them is to remember, to be reminded, to look to the future with hope. To listen to them is to open ourselves empathetically to the stories of others.

Every few months my family travel to the north of England to stay with my wife's sister and her family in Newcastle. Whenever we do we make a point of visiting the Cumberland Arms, a small and unassuming pub in Byker, a suburb in the east of the city. Aside from the good beer and a log fire, what marks the Cumberland Arms out is its generous approach to music. There are live gigs from local and visiting acts but, more often than not, there are also nights when anyone and everyone can simply bring an instrument and join in. No one leads. Instead, the latent song-knowledge of those present is explored and people simply join in with what they know, and listen and learn from what they don't. Ukuleles, guitars, violins and harmonicas all rise and fall in the mix with the human voice, and just as the beer flows, so does a warming spirit of acceptance and empathy in this sharing of music that relies so little on the ego.

In addition to forgiveness then, I'd propose music like this as approaching the ideal gift. Those who play are artists of the invisible, offering something with very little additional cargo. It is worship, though none of us would dare say it, nor dare denominate the god that the one sitting next to us is hallowing.

Beyond forgiveness and music, I also want to argue that feasting can be seen as an ideal gift too, and that the feast stands in contrast to the popular notion of Christian hospitality which, for Derrida and others, raises problems similar to that associated with gift.

Imagine a church running a soup kitchen for the homeless. In order to be able to offer this sort of hospitality we need to have a place where we can be hospitable. We need to have food we can spare, and time. The implication of soup-kitchen hospitality is thus that we are more powerful than those we are giving to. However, to give this up, to renounce any claim to property, to relinquish any sense of mastery over those we want to be hospitable to would ultimately mean we could not act as host, and nor could anyone else. There would be no hospitality at all.

Does this mean that hospitality is, like the perfect contentless gift, impossible? I believe not, and against the soup kitchen model of hospitality – where food is distributed as a one-way gift – I want to propose the feast. In the classic idea of a soup kitchen the servers prepare and serve the food, doling out ladles into bowls and handing over hunks of bread to people waiting in line. In contrast, at the feast we eat together, and it is this shared experience of food that serves to minimise the self, and thus the temptation to see the food as a power-play. As John Milbank notes from the German Catholic philosopher Robert Spaemann, 'in the feast egotism is mitigated, since here one eats only if one eats along with others'. Importantly, however, when we are at a feast *we do eat*. In other words, we are nourishing the self, but doing so in a manner that is also about eradicating the ego from the self.

Again we return to the desert and Jesus' temptation to turn stones to bread. By doing so he would be providing for the poor, but, we might reflect, in a manner more akin to a soup kitchen. Instead, Jesus feasts with the people. He takes a gift so small it might as well be invisible: five small loaves and a couple of fish for a crowd of thousands, gives thanks and feasts with them. He symbolically lifts the bread and fish to heaven – thus taking it away from any human claim to own it, and then draws it back down and distributes it, symbolising the gift returning from God to us. Here we see why giving thanks before a meal is so vital to the act of hospitality: *it removes what we have before us from our ownership*, and thus serves to balance the power relations that might be latent in our giving. When we feast what we are giving is not even ours to give; we are all receiving God's hospitality.

It is to such a feast that we look forward. Jesus' metaphor of heaven as a feast of the resurrected is apt for many reasons. We have seen in the previous section how Levinas has helped us see death as a ground for acting selflessly and ethically, and that the hope of resurrection might well contaminate that with self-interest. He is right: to act generously to the other simply in the hope that it will lead to eternal life is to tarnish that generosity irreversibly. Again, we should permit ourselves hope of resurrection, but not live focused on a presumption of it. If it comes it will be a gift, not a repayment for any action on our part. As such, it will deserve a feast.

So it is that as we prepare feasts and music for others now we do so in the spirit of becoming 'artists of the invisible' – offering all that we have and are to God, allowing it out of our sight and ownership, and thus receiving it back as a gift to share that we can all be thankful for. As in food, so in life: 'to give, to be good, is already to be resurrected.'[10]

Jesus' act of feeding thousands of people offers us a model of how to engage generously with others while minimising the power-imbalances and narcissism that could come from dramatic displays of food distribution. We have seen that to act in love for the other will require us to reflect on who we are as complex personalities in an increasingly fractured and technologically driven world. It will also require us to reflect on God as both separate from us and bound to us – and thus lead us to a healthy view of self and other that affirms both our individuality and interdependence. This healthy view will acknowledge our separation from and binding to the tools and technologies that we create and crave, and will urge us to spend time considering how best to use them in a balanced, as opposed to compromised way.

I have also argued that as we come to engage the other we need to do so as maturing selves and that our aim in life ought not to be becoming a hero – doing brave battle on behalf of those less powerful than us – but becoming an heir – one who sees themselves as part of a long line of hands into which and from which the gift will flow.

Following Henri Nouwen, the metaphor I used for this was parenthood: 'No father or mother ever became father or mother without having been son or daughter, but every son and daughter has to consciously choose to step beyond their childhood and become father and mother for others.'[11]

Nouwen himself, as I have pointed out, was a Catholic priest: his own opportunities for becoming a biological parent were always going to be very limited, yet he very clearly became, through his work with L'Arche, someone who consciously chose to step beyond childhood and become a parent for others. In this work he was being an agent of care, someone who could love and nurture others and bring them to a point of maturity themselves. His life's work was therefore deeply connected to the principle of hospitality, and thus intimately involved in the cycle of gift.

Part of the struggle with the metaphor of parenthood is with the power-relations that it dredges up from our own experiences, not only of being parented, but also of being schooled, of being involved with adults. No one likes to be patronised (yet I am amazed at how many are desperate for patronage) and it is this feeling of someone looking down on you, of having an undeserved authority over you, that sours people's feelings towards leadership in the church, and authority structures in general. How then can we work towards being good spiritual parents, without being patronising? It is the same problem that Derrida saw in the gift: how can we be generous, without implying that we are more powerful?

The unknotting of this problem comes from our understanding of our own place within history and within God. Just as at the feast we sit and give thanks for food together, and thus confer any ownership of the gift onto God, then as parents we freely acknowledge and remember not only our own lineage and history as children, but also constantly recognise our status as 'adopted children' in God's family. Our lineage is complex, our conception difficult, our relations with our divine parent tempestuous and evolving, yet bound tight with love.

The political philosopher Michael Sandel has called for us 'to appreciate children as gifts [and] accept them as they come, not as objects of our design or products of our will or instruments of our ambition'.[12] Moreover, quoting the theologian William May, he declares that parenthood, more than other human relationships, teaches us an 'openness to the unbidden'. It is this openness to surprise and rupture that roots parenthood – biological and metaphorical – firmly in the gift, and mitigates any temptation to see ourselves as parents in authority while forgetting that we too have been children, and all of us together are within the realm of the unbidden. If we are to become 'father and mother to others' we will need to remain within the generous spirit of gift, and doing so will require us to be wise, gracious and pragmatic – virtues that all parents strive for.

I have emphasised gift over commerce for good reason, and the example of food is once again pertinent. When I go to the supermarket to buy food I am swapping one form of goods for another: I take food home, but leave them with money – a sort of commodity potential which they can then exchange for something else as and when they please.[13] This sort of commercial transaction leaves the scales entirely balanced. The gift on the other hand, problematic as it is, leaves the scales unbalanced and thus carries with it a potential for further movement. To continue the food analogy, if I invite someone round for dinner, or prepare a feast, then it would be unthinkable for someone to offer to pay for the meal at the end. By leaving the scales unbalanced the gift of a meal opens the way for relationship to be deepened – a fact that the church offer-ing free burgers was exploiting. However, it is also important for the person giving the gift to consider what sort of meal the person coming would like. So we can see that gift exchange can work to enrich relationships in two ways: we are forced to consider who is the other that we are offering something to in order to make sure that what we give is appropriate, and the act of offering a gift – even though we must expect nothing in return – leaves a potential for further engagement at a later date. Gifts and relationships are self-affirming. Relationships are deepened by generous acts, but generous acts are deepened by relationship and understanding between giver and receiver.

Temporality

Love for others then must not only be rooted in generosity, but wise to the complexities that gift exchange brings. Yet it must also be fully prepared to engage in the arena of market exchange too, and not rush to judge the commercial sphere as a barren place where no engagement is possible, as a story related by the Polish correspondent Ryszard Kapuscinski confirms:

> In the early 1990s I was in Liberia, where there was a civil war, and I went to the front line with a unit of government troops. The front ran along a river, whose banks were joined at that spot by a bridge. Next to the bridge, on the govern-ment side there was a large market. On the other side of the river, occupied by Charles Taylor's rebels, there was nothing, just empty fields. On this front along the river, the mortars roared away and the shooting went on until midday. But in the afternoon peace reigned, and the rebels came over the bridge to go shopping at the market. On the way they handed their weapons over to a government patrol, which gave them back when they returned to their side with the goods they had

bought at the market. And so in a place of armed, bloody conflict there was simultaneously the exchange of produce and other goods.[14]

Market-places such as this one in Liberia act as public spaces in which transactions can occur. But, as St Paul well knew, this commercial exchange of goods also creates an environment in which other exchanges can take place. When he travelled to Athens, it was to the market-place that Paul went, knowing that that was where the philosophers gathered – not because they were there to buy and sell ideas, but because the natural commercial flow provided the best place to engage people in conversation too.

Of course, markets can only give rise to other forms of exchange when they are perceived to be fair. If the government forces in Liberia were encouraging traders to charge exorbitant prices to the rebels then the market would not be a place of peace for long. But what is most interesting about the peace that broke out daily is that it was a *temporary* peace, just as the music that strikes up at the Cumberland Arms is only a temporary music, just as the feeding of 5,000 people with five loaves and two fish was a temporary feast. In all of these situations, after a short time of respite, the waves of normal service roll back: warfare, noise, hunger.

The temporal nature of these moments runs against the culture of permanence that runs right through the Church. We speak of eternity, of an undying body of Christ, of the constancy of our witness in stone cathedrals that appear to have been there since the dawn of time. Our unending prayers end with 'forever and ever, Amen'; our song and liturgy hang heavy, invested with hundreds of years of history. Tradition is good. It can be a healthy momentum that carries us straight when the winds of change blow hard. But central to our tradition is the story of a man whose ministry lasted but three years. He had the choice – he could have sustained a far longer time with his followers, could have delayed his necessary death for many years. Instead, he allowed himself to be cut off. What then is it about the temporary that is to be celebrated?

The history of the Church (and connectedly much of the modern history of the US in particular) is littered with examples of small groups of believers trying to create utopian spaces – perfect, idealised societies based on their version of godly principles. The utopian vision usually runs like this: a community becomes more and more obsessed with the impurity and sinfulness of the world around it, and withdraws to some isolated place to build a new world, which, rooted in the pure word of God, will be perfect – and thus eternal.

In an article reviewing John Gray's book *Black Mass*, which examines how dangerous utopian ideas were in the twentieth century, Anthony Dworkin notes that 'their guiding inspiration is that conflict and coercion can be finessed away by a correct reordering of society ... but they cannot fulfil their objectives without attempting to remake human nature, or eliminate groups within society that are seen as agents of corruption or reaction'.[15] He then goes on to argue that 'the real harm came in the 20th Century, when utopians abandoned the idea of withdrawing from the world and instead attempted to remake it'.

We have already explored the two reflexes we experience in the face of having to meet the other: hiding away in our castles or fleeing to other lands. We can now see that that within the mission of the church we have tried to work these out through two impulses: withdrawing from the world in an attempt to create perfect mini-heavens on earth, and attempting to remake the world. The closed-off monasteries were examples of the former, the Crusades and conquests examples of the latter. The former abandoned the rest of the world to its fate, while the latter used violence to force the new order into being.

We can see the utopian ideal then as covering two connected urges: to cleanse either ourselves and our immediate local community from sin in the case of withdrawal, or a whole country or society from impurity or dictatorship in the case of remaking. This cleansing urge is spurred on by the belief that *if only we could expunge this one last bit of dirt*, then an eternally good, new world would be born and an era of everlasting peace would come.

In more recent times thinkers like Michel Foucault have theorised about 'heterotopias' – 'other spaces' which societies or individuals create, within which we confine deviance or difference in order to sustain our utopian ideals. A prison is one such place: it has not tried to destroy or eliminate the evil of society, but rather has removed them to another place, in the hope that that removal would permit the rest to continue to live in perfect peace.

These idealised places then are intimately connected with the dirt boundaries that we establish in an attempt to order the world. The problem with them is that they neglect to understand the basic problem of human nature: that we are never going to be perfect people, and any purified community, no matter how faultless its founders, will always produce dirt and deviance of its own.

We are faced then with a similar paradox to that presented by the gift: do we give up on generosity altogether, on any attempt to create just and peaceful communities and a just and peaceful world, or do we throw our whole lives at attempts to attain this unreachable perfection and very probably resort to violence and bloody revolution in our quest for it?

Both positions are based on a similar premise. Giving up on the possibility that anything can ever be good is to take a view that nothing can ever change. Working tirelessly for the purity of a community or principle is to take a view that if, just for a moment, total purity can be achieved, then nothing will ever infect it again and an eternal utopia will be established.

Again, we must seek balance rather than compromise, and Dworkin outlines what a middle position might look like by examining Jay Winter's idea of 'minor utopias'. Winter's book *Dreams of Peace and Freedom* describes these places as ones that 'sketch out a world very different from the one we live in, but from which not all social conflict or all oppression has been eliminated'.

It is in the light of this description that I think we can gain a new perspective on these moments of feasting, these evenings of liberating music, and these stories of Jesus' miracles in his very short ministry. In each of these examples we can see that they carry hints of 'a world very different from the one we live in', while not attempting to be permanent statements or manifestations of that new world order, and certainly not attempting to eliminate all social conflict or oppression. Jesus fed 5,000 people, but only for one afternoon. Arms may be put down while fruit and vegetables are purchased, but only until the market is over and hostilities begin again.

Penetration and cartography

The anarchist writer Hakim Bey has described these 'minor' or 'dirty' utopias as TAZ – 'Temporary Autonomous Zones'.[16] Bey's essay on TAZ has become something of a classic. He begins it with an exploration of the eighteenth-century 'pirate utopias' which sprang up around the world in an 'information network' that gave access to remote hideouts, illegal trading stations – 'whole mini societies living consciously outside the law and determined to keep it up, even if only for a short but merry life'.[17] These were (very) minor utopias, places that sprang up and died quickly. They had to be so because the territories they were using were sovereign places, under the control of states.

Because of the basic nature of communication technologies at the time, it was impossible for states like Britain to keep proper tabs on all of the far-flung corners of its vast empire. Bey writes of the final 'closure of the map' in 1899, when the last remaining piece of Earth was claimed by a nation-state. Since then there has been 'no more *terra incognita*', 'not one square inch of Earth goes unpoliced or untaxed . . . in theory'.[18] In other words, the British had their maps, detailed descriptions of the places they ruled and the tax they could expect to levy from them, but the reality on the ground, away from the map, was often different simply because of the vast distances between London and these islands.

It was into these gaps between the maps held by the empirical rulers and the reality on the ground that pirates and other insurrectionists fled. Until they were reported, until the troops could be mustered and the ships stocked and sent sailing half way round the new world to flush them out, these corsairs enjoyed total autonomy, living lives outside of the strictures of the Queen's law and the taxman's book.

Bey then moves away from piracy (though we shall return to it later) and translates the principle of these 'unmapped places' into the language of personal and social transformation. As an anarchist Bey is naturally sceptical about the power of authority structures to effect positive change. What he sees in TAZ is a way of giving people quick glimpses of what a new world might look like, infecting them with a counter-cultural vision of a different order which disappears before the authorities have time to come in and destroy it. TAZ, he says, is 'like an uprising which does not engage directly with the State, a guerrilla operation which liberates an area (of land, of time, of imagination) and then dissolves itself to re-form elsewhere/elsewhen, before the State can crush it.'[19] The 'rave' scene of the late 1980s and early 1990s was a good example of this. Word spread virally (without mobiles or email, of course) about where a rave would be happening, and people would turn up and dance as long and hard as they could before the police came in and turned the power off.

TAZ is not simply about the battle against state power; its principles can be equally applied to resistance to all forms of social control, and once recognised, can be spied in many different areas of life. For example, the Greenbelt festival in the UK sees around 20,000 people, mostly from a Christian tradition, gather at a large horse-racing course for four days of talks, theatre, debate, film, justice-making and music. Over those four days the land is 'liberated' – it is no longer a racecourse – and those attending are given a taste of how the world might be different. As Bey describes it, TAZ 'envisions an intensification of everyday life, or as the Surrealists might have said, life's penetration by the Marvellous.'[20]

As I shared a meal with Christians, Jews and Muslims – English, Israeli and Palestinian – in Bethlehem, in a restaurant in the shadow of the 'security wall', this temporary breaking through of a new world is what we all felt.

As we took over dead church spaces and transformed them with projections and installations and, just for a few hours, filled them with strange poetry, this penetration of life by something marvellous was what we felt in the Vaux community I was a part of.

And this is precisely what we see in Jesus' miracles: an intensification of the everyday as a huge catch of fish is hauled after a barren night, life's penetration by the marvellous as food is multiplied and wine overflows from water jars. Indeed, we can read the whole incarnation event in the same way – a divine life existing in intense festival for a few brief years before the authorities caught it on radar and tried to crush it.

Those in power, those sent out to make maps and codify the power structures of the day, will hardly notice these alternative topographies, these small folds in the creases of their maps. They are lands hidden away in coves, their meaning dressed in innocent parables. I want to argue, however, that these Temporary Autonomous Zones are precisely the places within which we can best engage the 'other', and that if as people of faith we are going to seek out how we might follow Jesus' command to love our neighbours, then we need to think about how our expressions of church can be moved from ones informed by permanence and utopianism, to ones informed by TAZ.

The question we must immediately ask of these spaces is whether they are simply cruel. By their temporality, are they just offering a fleeting glimpse of a different arrangement of the world before returning people to the grim reality of the status quo, or do they hold within them some more mysterious seeds, from which lasting change might grow? Was Jesus raising expectations unfairly when he fed those 5,000 people? They were given lunch – couldn't he also have provided for their supper? If they had followed him the next day, another day when their economic circumstances hadn't changed, shouldn't he have provided for them again?

Similar questions could be asked about festivals. If Greenbelt is so good for those four days, why not make it a permanent event? The 70s hit by the British band Wizzard is repeated endlessly at parties every December: 'I wish it could be Christmas every day.' But do we really? The few feet of snow in London was wonderful for a few days; would the wonder have remained had it been a permanent fixture?

As soon as we trample on it, the pure white snow soon turns to dirty slush and ice. Fun as it is to spend four days in a tent with little sleep, make-shift toilets and a whole lot of hastily boiled pasta, it is not a life many who come to Greenbelt would want to live permanently.

The questions surrounding Jesus' miraculous feeding of the crowd soon become equally complicated. If he were to continue this as a daily event, would it have to be restricted to those who were there for the original miracle? If so, who would check? What would happen to those who made a living from making bread or catching fish if Jesus continued to undercut their sales by this miraculous multiplication? Would he still have to be there today, feeding a population of six billion and more with free food? What sort of people would that make us into, and what sort of God would it be that we were worshipping?

It seems that there is an essential element of temporality in miracles, and this element extends down from the miraculous to the marvellous and plain hospitable too. Imagine throwing a feast for those disadvantaged in your community. How many should you cater for? Should there be a limit on numbers? The 'spiritual' answer would be that there should be no limits: we should not turn anyone away, and we should give sacrificially until all are fed. The question again comes about what we should do when the next meal comes around. These same people are perhaps still unemployed, still with little access to good food – so should we be feeding them *every* day? If we did this, and it would seem that it would be a perfectly good 'Christian' response to do so, what effect would it have on our own family lives? What impact would it have on the local economy?

These are questions that Derrida and others were alive to. In *The Gift of Death* Derrida noted that 'I cannot respond to the call, the request, the obligation, or even the love of another, without sacrificing the other other, the other others . . .'[21] In other words, whenever I try to help one 'other', I am turning my help away from 'another other', and thus my desire to have equal compassion on everybody ends in paradox. Milbank picks up the same problem, writing that when we try to be hospitable, 'our responsibilities tend to become unlimited because we owe our lives infinitely to every other person [so] no one could ever legitimately relax and enjoy the benefits of the sacrifices of others. Thus the only thing that is achieved is the continued carrying out of self-obliteration.'[22]

By clarifying from the outset that the spaces we are creating are temporary, we may, in fact, be ensuring that they are more long-lasting. If we set out bold plans for utopian places where the hungry are all fed and there is no pain or conflict, we are destining them for disappointment and collapse as those involved burn out, or those close to them are starved of love. The poverty, hunger and injustice around our world is plain to see. What should our response be to these huge problems? Do we throw ourselves at them with no thought for 'the other others' we have responsibility for, or do we say that no one can ever feed and clothe them all and lift them out of poverty, and do nothing?

The beauty of TAZ is that it injects hope into these overpowering situations. The forces at work against us are huge. The powerful own the maps and have legislated for every last inch. But in the interstitial spaces, under the radar of those who would want to configure the world for their own benefit, brief festivals of hope are taking place. They are temporary flashes of light in dark places, but long after they have gone the air hangs heavy with a generous odour, and those who thought they saw something different are, in miniscule ways, penetrated by the marvellous for a second and can never quite get rid of that feeling. 'Hush,' says the Church, leaving its petrified walls and tiptoeing mischievously toward the public square, 'I am doing a new thing. Do you not perceive it?'

The sun rises

Be gone cobwebs,
dust, don't gather.
air, don't still
and stones don't settle.

All that creeps and steals,
skulks, sneaks and slithers,
should retreat now,
for there is life here, reignited,
burning, heat and light.

Though no word can yet be said,
a stone still cries out,
and retreats in holy fear.

Air rushes in terror to escape,
but is inhaled again,
in, out, in, out.
A leaden chest rises, and falls;
black blood melts red and circulates.
an eye is opened,
a muscle twitches.

A word is about to be said.
Creation, three days in revolution,
waits in cold dread for its hearing
but receives only forgiveness
and feels only warmth as
the sun rises.

Tacticians and strategists

All of us who are passionate about following Christ have to be interested in perceiving this new thing because newness is an integral part of the story of our faith. The incarnation was a radically new breaking-in of God to our experience and frailty. The resurrection was a new breaking-out of God from the strictures of religion. Peter's vision in Acts 10 was, for him, a completely new way of thinking about the way God was including people in salvation. Each of these breakthroughs had to be perceived and interpreted by faithful seekers: a young girl, eastern astrologers and passionate fishermen. But, while many of these perceptions turned out to be good interpretations of what God was mysteriously doing, some have turned out to be rather poor.

Judas was, I would argue, trying to faithfully perceive what God wanted when he attempted to catalyse a revolution that would have seen Jesus overthrow the Romans and be installed as a Messiah-King in Jerusalem. He was wrong. Paul was trying to faithfully perceive what God wanted when, against the advice of others, he returned to Jerusalem in what could be seen as a deliberate ploy to get himself arrested and shipped off to Rome. In both these cases, as I have argued earlier, I believe we see two people attempting to *strategise* for change. Judas is a zealot. One interpretation of his surname 'Iscariot' is 'member of the Sicarii' or 'Dagger Men', a group of ultra-zealots who were determined to overthrow the Roman occupation by assassinations and terrorism.[23] Paul's history is steeped in Pharisaism, and though his writings are full of wonderful expositions of the supremacy of grace above law, they are still writings that carry a heavy sense of instruction, of telling people exactly what to do.

Jesus neither led a revolution, nor wrote a book of instructions on how to live. I believe this was because he understood perfectly that the way to beat the domination system is never to face it down. He could have come to earth with a billion angels and a squadron of fiery chariots; instead Mary was, in the theo-sexual sense, 'penetrated by the Marvellous' as a tiny seed was planted within her. Jesus' incarnation and ministry thus present us with the final critique of strategic religion; on the cross, where we see God almost deliberately 'lose' – as if duped into being strung up by a scheming, fearful group of clerics – we see the end of power games. God will not play.

I sincerely believe that if the Church allows itself to be tied up in strategies, into 'winning' people for Christ, it will end inexorably moving towards power-politics, towards support for wars, and away from genuine concern for the 'other'.

Isn't having no strategy a strategy in itself? If we meant by strategy having any kind of planning or forethought, yes, but I want to use the word in the sense that the Jesuit turned social scientist and philosopher Michel de Certeau does. He sees strategy as a form of authority that is capable of producing laws. Those involved in strategy are attempting to perpetuate ideas and institutions by the things that they produce. Strategists therefore need to be heavily resourced, and are always interested in imposing order. Instead, he proposes 'tactics', which are used by those who defy authority and infiltrate institutions, but do not wish to take them over. Tacticians, unlike strategists, operate far more frugally, with no specific headquarters, yet are capable of assembling groups, as the context requires them, very swiftly.

In these terms I have no problem critiquing Paul and Judas as strategists. Judas was a revolutionary who wanted to take over. Paul wanted to build capacity in centres of power. I believe that these sorts of strategic approaches have left a harmful legacy in the Church, one that has overshadowed the TAZ-tactician that we see in Jesus' ministry.

A church that is aiming to truly be a 'body of Christ' will then, I believe, be one that abandons careful strategy and instead embarks on a tactical adventure from one eruption of TAZ to another. It will be a church that has no interest in 'taking over' or formulating models by which others can perpetuate what it is doing. Instead, acting within the frugal economy of gift and without access to great resources, it will consist of a complex network of believers 'capable of swiftly combining according to current necessity' who are ready to create festive, hospitable, healing and creative places in the folds of the dominant cartography – places that will dissolve as quickly as they were erected, which, like the lover in Song of Songs, leave those touched by them aching to know more.

These places will be temporary not because of lack of commitment – and it is vital to appreciate this in a society plagued by non-commitment – but because it is in these temporal spaces, where everyday life is intensified, that we can best begin to engage the other in a way that will lead to long-term transformation. We will see later that this doesn't mean that permanence has no place, but it does mean that we need to be very aware that a desire for permanence can lead to violence – either to the self, through burnout, or to those 'other others' around us whom we sacrifice in order to fulfil our service.

Nomads and travellers

Our natural human condition is caught between temporality and permanence. We build huge stone cities, but rarely put down roots. We appear all to be, by nature, nomadic. The Liberian fighters are none other than us: laying down our daily battles for a moment wherever we can find refreshment, before raising our defences again and marching out into the night.

We dare not stay long at these occasional feasts, and it is better that they do not last forever. Why? Because we are all so far from Eden. Unadulterated, naked communion frightens us. Pushed onto the road to the East, we have become used to the journey, travelling from place to place, negotiating the narrow path of suspicion of those we meet along the way, yet fascinated by what they can teach us.

Travelling around Britain I have become more aware recently of the etymology of the names of places. So many of them are rooted in confluence: Oxford, the ford across the river Ox; Cambridge, the bridge over the river Cam; Exmouth, the mouth of the Exe. Those that are not connected to rivers are still often compound words, forged together where one place or thing meets an-other. We stop at these meeting places for a while, but we know deep down that we are between the now and the not yet, that we are not yet home, and move on.

In these short stops, where we gather briefly with others, we share stories and pick up hints of the place we are heading. It seems that it was meant this way; we are on a sojourn from heaven, a learning journey, and must keep travelling until we are called back, all the while listening out for what we can divine from those we meet.

In *The Other*, a philosophical meditation on his life as a jour-nalist in foreign places, Ryszard Kapuscinski reflects that:

> for me the world has always been a great Tower of Babel. However, it is a tower in which God has mixed not just the languages but also the cultures and customs, passions and interests, and whose inhabitant He has made into an ambiva-lent creature combining the Self and non-Self, himself and the Other, his own and the alien.[24]

This road we are on is thus an endlessly fascinating place, a place of infinite discovery, just as it is also of self-discovery. But it can only be so if we are prepared to stop, put down our weapons, and engage with the other.

Reflecting on what Levinas was trying to say in all of his philo-sophical writings, Kapuscinski goes on: ' "Stop," he seems to be saying to the man hurrying along in the rushing crowd. "There beside you is another person. Meet him . . . Look at the Other's face as he offers it to you. Through this face he shows you your-self: more than that – he brings you closer to God." '[25]

I see myself in this figure, 'hurrying on to a receding future', as R. S. Thomas would have it, hurrying but desperate for someone to stop me and look into my face, to bring me closer to God. The cities we have built, these huge stone tools we have crafted, seem purposed to help us avoid confrontation with the other, even as we are crammed closer and closer to one another in crowded streets and commuting carriages. This is the paradox of urban life: proximity to so many, but communion with so few. Capitalism drives us together – specialisation of labour and economies of scale – and consumerism drives us apart. We lower our heads and push on into the crowds.

Like all nomads, when we do meet others on the road, when we raise our heads and catch their eyes and stop, we need ways to work out each other's identity. Kapuscinski points out that in traditional African nomadic tribes this would be done through a long and careful exchange of questions, both parties trying to work out which tribe and clan the other was from, and whether relations with those groups were good or not. We have not moved on from this much, and have simply introduced a whole range of shortcuts which allow us to announce our identities very quickly: what we are wearing, which phone we are carrying, which bar we are drinking in, which films we are watching, which books and newspapers we are decreasingly reading. All of these are like Post-Its on our bodies, allowing others to speedily decode whether we are good liberals or well read or Apple users or indie kids or EMOs or ravers. With so many interactions between ourselves and others each day in the city, these unspoken signals are vital to our sanity. We can quickly work out whether someone is 'one of us' or not, and adjust our defences accordingly.

What this strategy achieves, of course, is ghettoism. Our cities become stratified multiverses, parallel dimensions living alongside one another, but only meeting when there is rupture between them: a banker takes a wrong turn into a dark street, a cleaner opens the door onto a board meeting. It is in these surprising moments that we suddenly become aware of the heights and depths and widths of difference that exist so close to us. What happens next is what we must take care to get right.

One option is to adopt the position of tourist. The tourist is a traveller who may, on first inspection, be indistinguishable from the nomads and gypsies who journey along life's road. But look closer, and we see that the tourist is actually the exact opposite. Jack Kerouac's 'Dean Moriarty' is no tourist. The tourist travels with an attitude of observing a spectacle, while the road-tripper's aim is to disappear completely into that spectacle. As Bey notes in another essay, 'the tourist consumes difference',[26] they exploit otherness. By reframing the impoverished other as 'exotic' the tourist is able to fetishise the difference between themselves and those they see begging on the streets, and convince themselves that they have no responsibility for them.

It is not that travelling is wrong. Tourism was established in the nineteenth century as a way of making money out of the exotic species the Brits had discovered in their empirical conquests. It carried with it all that sense of power and supremacy, but preceding it was a fine tradition of pilgrimage and exploration, of going to engage with and meet others, rather than observe them from a suitably sanitised and air-conditioned distance.

Love for our neighbours means refusing to fetishise the ways that they are different to us. When we encounter the other on the road, we must resist the position of tourist, resist the warped power-relations and patronising offering of soup-kitchen help and seek to meet them eye to eye as fellow travellers. As Christians in particular, as those whose lives are being transformed by the incarnation, we must regain the ancient spirit of Cleopas and his companion as they walked from Jerusalem to Emmaus.

The beauty of this story lies in the hospitality that each showed to the other. Walking on a road together was important for security, but one still had to be wary of who one walked with. When Jesus comes alongside them and joins their conversation they are clearly wary – here is someone who appears to know nothing of the greatest news of the day – but they accept this stranger anyway and strike up with him. It is only later when they share a meal that their eyes are opened, the familiar symbol of the raised and broken bread raising their spirits and smashing their grief.

When we read this story we also need to bear in mind the culture within which it takes place, as well as the culture of the person who narrated it. The Jewish disciples would have been well-versed in the stories of the Old Testament about strangers on the road. Abraham's response of hospitality to the three visitors who passed his way on the road would have formed part of their own attitudes to such meetings. Luke, who wrote the Gospel in which the Emmaus story is told, was probably a Greek, and would therefore have been brought up with the legends of the anthropomorphic gods of ancient Greece. For both the narrator and the protagonists, the backdrop to this road-trip story is, as Kapuscinski puts it, 'a belief that no one could be sure if an approaching traveller, nomad or stranger were a man, or a god resembling a man'. And, he points out, 'This uncertainty, this intriguing ambivalence is one of the sources of the culture of hospitality, which recommends showing every form of kindness to newcomers.'[27]

Neither Luke nor the two disciples would have needed to look back quite so far into their history though, because Jesus made precisely this point in the final parable he told in Matthew 25:

> 'Lord, when did we see you hungry and feed you, or thirsty and give you something to drink? When did we see you a stranger and invite you in, or needing clothes and clothe you? When did we see you sick or in prison and go to visit you?'

> The King will reply, 'I tell you the truth, whatever you did for one of the least of these brothers of mine, you did for me.'

Herein lies a wonderful meditation on this separate and bound, immanent yet Other divine stranger that we pursue along the road. We appear never to see God, yet God is to be seen all around us. We appear to be able to do nothing in service of God, yet are constantly serving. Our Lover runs from us. Why? To hide away? No. God runs in order to become hidden in the others around us. God hides in the poor and the oppressed and the different and challenging precisely so that we might go in search of God – not as gawping tourists, but as pilgrims – and become strangers ourselves among them, finding love for them and God as we do so.

God is love. But God does not simply crave our love. God's craving is trinity: that we might love ourselves, and God and our neighbours equally. If God were so easily found, would we bother to look out for the poor? Would we not simply trample over them in our rushing toward heaven? God's hiding is not deliberate obstruction but an integral part of our maturing from self-centred Adams and Eves, blind even to each other's nudity, into loving human beings. God's incarnation into the divine stranger is a call for us to be shaken out of our comforts and become strangers too – that we might better see what it is to be on the fringes of society, and better understand how to love those we meet.

Sent from Eden as nomads until we have learned our lessons, God's constant re-incarnation into those we meet on the road demands that we are active participants in the pursuit of our Lover. It is no good for us to be sex-tourists: consuming difference, fetishising the other, abusing our power and riches in pretence that we are somehow 'expanding our horizons' or 'finding ourselves' on our travels. No. Matthew 25 and the Emmaus story demand that we quiet our sycophantic choruses of saccharine love, sung eyes shut and hands up high, and instead turn our voices to the poor, the oppressed, the homeless, the lonely and imprisoned and sing tough songs of love and action with our eyes meeting theirs and our hands held out in solidarity. The prophet Amos agrees.

> Away with the noise of your songs!
> I will not listen to the music of your harps.
> But let justice roll on like a river,
> righteousness like a never-failing stream![28]

Having eaten of the tree of the knowledge of good and evil, we must now learn to digest the depth of what it says. It says this:

'*The Other has a face, and it is a sacred book in which good is recorded.*'[29]

At the end of all things we read that the book of life will be opened, and the dead will be judged according to what they had done (see Rev. 20). Perhaps it won't be a ledger of our achievements, an inventory of our possessions or an encyclopaedia of our knowledge. It may simply be a book of photographs. 'Who are these people?' we might then ask. 'They are the faces of the others that you saw,' God might well reply. And the tourists who took snapshots will head left, and those who saw the faces, and put their cameras down and looked into their eyes, will head right.

Pirates and heretics

Somewhere ahead of us, behind us, around us, God is on the road, hiding among our neighbours. There is no divine cartography that can tell us precisely where. Maps are closed spaces, facsimiles and representations of the real world created by the powerful, by those who want to claim ownership, levy taxes and impose the law. The gazetteer is a closed book where all is documented, labelled, gridded, contoured and pinned down to perfect scale with a legend. There is no other interpretation.

But away from these maps, beyond even what Google Streetview can tell us, is a real world that is constantly under reconstruction and renegotiation. Here is a church, the map says. But we turn up to find only a building.

There can be no map of TAZ. We explored earlier in the chapter on the otherness of God that the role of the priest, rather than being a gatekeeper or spiritual cartographer, is to live in the 'dangerous place'. We can now see that this dangerous place is the place that cannot be mapped. There is no strategy that will protect us and give us exact directions to make our way through. There is only a tactic of love. Outside of the gated utopian communities that we have built to protect ourselves, Jesus still wanders. From time to time, in places we cannot triangulate and at times we cannot predict, he appears in the 'other'. For a short while life is intensified and penetrated by something marvellous. The map-makers hurry there with their instruments and inks, while others will be convinced that this must represent some special geography, and make permanent camp there, setting up shrines and outlining utopian visions. Both will be disappointed. The soldiers will come, but the pirates will have gone, the remnants of a feast still heavy in the air, their treasure hidden in a place that none will find.

As Bey discovered in his research, there is very little accurate history of pirate life. This is unsurprising. History is a document written and preserved by the powerful, and pirates were never much interested in power or preservation.

In his major work on the subject, *Pirate Utopias: Moorish Corsairs and European Renegadoes*, Bey sets out to explore what drove people to piracy and, in particular, why along the North African coastal trade routes of the Mediterranean so many of them seemed to have also converted to some form of Islam. From the short-lived pirate-run port of Salé, pirates sailed out to plunder the rich pickings of goods being transported around Europe from the Crusader lands in the Middle East and beyond.

As to why people turned to piracy, Bey makes it clear:

> Labour conditions in the merchant marines of Europe presented an abysmal picture of emerging capitalism at its worst – and conditions in European navies were even more horrendous. The sailor had to consider himself the lowest and most rejected figure of all European economy and government – powerless, underpaid, brutalised, tortured, lost to scurvy and storms at sea, the virtual slave of wealthy merchants and ship-owners, and of penny-pinching kings and greedy princes.[30]

For this reason, he argues, 'piracy must be studied as a form of social resistance'. Being a sailor-slave was so horrific that a short free life of plunder would have been very tempting. As for the

Islamic connection, this again appeared to be deliberate resistance against the powerful Christian empire that they served: 'I hate Europe, Europe hates Islam . . . Perhaps I might like Islam?'

Yet these sailors who turned to Islam and piracy were not necessarily the apostate thieves that the European historians made them out to be. Their conversion from merchant seaman to pirate, from Christian to Muslim was an act of social resistance against a capitalist, Christian Europe that had abused them so badly.

Let us be clear, I am not wanting to defend their thievery, nor the violence that they perpetrated.[31] However, it is important to see these acts in the context of merchants who were plundering far-off lands, often violently pillaging them for precious goods that they traded for fantastic profit – while paying those who sailed for them almost nothing. The empirical acts of European countries like France, Spain and Britain were not so different to theft, and the violent methods they used to establish trade routes were utterly horrendous.

At the same time, we also need to read what material there exists on piracy with caution, written as much of it was by Europeans who were losing money because of their actions. Other documents show that pirate culture embraced difference and diversity in a way that mainstream culture did not. As well as relieving ships of their precious cargoes of spices and other goods, pirates are also known to have attacked slave ships and freed all those on board.

In contrast to the fear and ignorance that characterised Europe's religion at the time, pirates – violent men, yes, just like their 'loyal' counterparts still in the navies – were liberal and accepting of other beliefs.

Pirates then, represented for mainstream Europeans something of a shadow, a dark inversion of all that they stood for. Living by thievery, free of repressive legal structures and enjoying life to the full, it seems perhaps that Jung would have sensed in the European governments' fanaticism to overthrow the pirates an overcompensation for doubts about the merits of their own society. With the proliferation of children's books on pirates, it seems that the same might still be true.

Those who turned 'Moorish corsairs' were branded not only violent thieves, but heretics too. Interestingly, Bey sees heresy as a vehicle for cultural transfer: 'When a religion of one culture permeates to another culture, it does so initially as "heresy" – only later do the Orthodox Authorities arrive and straighten everyone out and make them toe the line.'[32] But the map-makers and jurists again arrive too late: the infection has already taken hold. Bey sees this in the emergence of Celtic Christianity, which initially absorbed a great deal of Druidry. Once the Celtic Christians had been pulled back into line, a wonderful cross-fertilisation had already taken place: Christianity had been introduced into Celtic culture, but Celtic culture had also been introduced into Christianity.

In this way we can read something of the Trickster into Bey's descriptions of pirates. Lewis Hyde's summary of what dirty tricksters do is clear enough: 'As a rule, Trickster takes a god who lives on high and debases him or her with earthly dirt – or appears to debase, for in fact the usual consequence of this dirtying is the god's eventual renewal.'[33]

Thus, projected as filthy, thieving heretics by mainstream European society, pirates may actually have been functioning as vital bridgeheads into beliefs and principles that were too radical and dangerous for European minds to accept. Yet by continuing to be fascinated by them, and by branding their beliefs as heretical, they were actually planting the seeds of these desperately needed changes, which only came to proper fruition in the work of the abolitionists, fair-trade campaigners and inter-faith dialoguers. Thus, pirates, to use Peter Rollins' language, function as 'orthodox heretics': their actions are condemned by those in authority as heresy, but this heresy is later embraced as orthodoxy.

We can see this cycle occurring in the music business. In the 1960s 'pirate' radio stations were moored off the coast of Britain and broadcast new-fangled pop music to the nation's youth. Those in the establishment were spitting mad, and passed legislation to try to stop them. When it became clear that this was impossible, the BBC, the very bastion of the establishment, created 'Radio 1', which would play this cursed pop music, and hired most of the DJs off the pirate boats to become presenters. In the same way, more recently we have seen the piratical heresy of Napster – a free music downloading service that was condemned as criminal by every music label under the sun – reincarnated in the orthodoxy of Spotify – a free music streaming service that music labels say may save their businesses.

What might any of this mean for us as we seek to love the other? In a world where established, politically powerful Christianity is being rejected by people in droves, and where the economic structures that reward failed bankers with millions are being similarly questioned by those who lose their jobs because of them, I want to make a plea for Christian piracy. In acts of radical social resistance, people who were the lowest of the low, those who had been exploited by the rich and powerful and religious of their day, rejected the world as mapped out by the Empire, and created a more wild, more inclusive, more dangerous one. This is not Blackbeard, Jack Sparrow or Long John Silver. This is the gospel. In Temporary Autonomous Zones, in the 'minor utopias' that Jesus and his followers created, we get hints of genuine hospitality coming through the overtones of violence that ruled the day.

Seventeenth-century Europe was, in psychological terms 'blocked'. Repressed by class boundaries, suffering 'future shock' due to the radical changes that overseas expansion brought, and following a religion that co-opted God into empire-construction and, as we read in the Salem Witch Trials of 1692, cursed the different, it is no surprise that pirates appeared on the high seas. They represented then, and Jung might say still represent now, the beginnings of the unblocking. Their radical freedom and rejection of the heavy hand of the law saw them cursed as heretics by the authorities, but written into legend by the people.

This is perhaps why piracy continues to fascinate us. Pirates offer us a glimpse into a world that is more free and less bound to the drudgery of the rat-race. In 1724, in the shadow of St Paul's Cathedral in London, a small leather-bound book was placed on sale next to the fine illuminated religious texts of the day. Captain Charles Johnson's *A General History of the Robberies and Murders of the most notorious Pyrates* was an instant success. From the shores of the Thames – where pirates were strung up on gibbets for all to see their treachery – Johnson's readers would have been able to dream of an existence that was not permanently in the shadow of the imposing cathedral church that overlooked them. In the book they could revel in the words of one Captain Mission, who, having captured a Dutch slave ship off the coast of Africa, made a long speech to its crew, declaring that: 'The Trading for those of our Species cou'd never be agreeable to the Eyes of divine Justice and that no Man has the Power of the Liberty of another; and while those who profess a more enlightened Knowledge of the Deity, sold men like Beasts; they prov'd that their Religion was no more than a Grimace!'[34] It is time for this pirate spirit of Captain Mission to shake our faith again.

In our overtime culture, our endless consumerism and constant upgrade mindset, in our shackles to debt and silent acceptance of the erosion of our human rights, we are becoming a 'blocked' culture again. Too many of us have become the 'virtual slaves of wealthy merchants and ship-owners, and of penny-pinching kings and greedy princes'.

With our every move covered by CCTV, our every click monitored by government agencies, our lives narrowed by what we are told we can believe, the flows within and beyond us are reduced to a trickle. In other words, we are falling out of love. With rising depression, addiction, obesity and mental ill-health we are falling out of love with ourselves. With fundamentalism and constant arguments over sexuality and battles for numbers we are falling out of love with God. And with knife crime and school massacres and racism and fears over asylum and economic protectionism we are falling out of love with those we perceive are different to us and pose a threat to us.

When people, religion and society become blocked in this way, it is time for some rebellion. First-century Judaism, tied up in Phariseeism, oppressed by occupation and obsessed with purity required an uneducated heretic to rise up and unblock it so that 'the ongoing process of development could unfold once more'. Seventeenth-century Europe needed the pirates to rise up and force a fresh evaluation of faith, justice and liberty. And now, in our world blocked by cynicism, consumerism and rationalism it is time again for the scurvied sailors in the pews to rise up in proper Christian piracy, celebrate the one strung up on a gibbet and declare themselves free people as, with music and feasting, they set slaves free.

This is church as TAZ: a generous, hospitable place that defies cartography and rejects closed-circuitry. Away from the gaze of CCTV here are places that will once again be places of refuge, places where civil liberties are not just taken seriously but where civilians can feel liberated, where kings can come down from their lonely castles, rubber ball in hand and join us, for a while, playing in the snow.

'Come on in!' waves the minister from the door of a church in a cartoon I saw recently. 'Come on out!' waves the man in the street, beckoning him to leave the safety of his stone church. This is the constant challenge of the incarnation. If we are to be the body of Christ and follow Jesus' instruction to love God and our neighbours it is as if we have to appear to love God less: we have to leave the safe sanctuary of divine contemplation and be born again as strangers among those we want to serve. In this newly born state we must hold up these twin values of generosity and temporality, knowing that we can only give because we ourselves have received, conscious that our work will not be permanent because we refuse the way of violence.

Face to face with the other

Early on in this book I quoted the theologian Miroslav Volf, who urged in his book *Exclusion and Embrace* that theologians should 'concentrate less on social arrangements, and more on fostering the kind of social agents capable of . . . creating just, truthful and peaceful societies'.[35] We should not focus on structures and strategies but on shaping a cultural climate in which such social agents will thrive.

The question, of course, is how: how can we help people to love God, themselves and their neighbours better? What I believe Volf is getting at is that no amount of careful social construction is, on its own, going to create a peaceful society. No matter what wonderful housing we build for people, what social services we fund, what democratic institutions we create and no matter how brilliant our church programmes, people are not going to grow into truth and justice unless there are social agents to model such change.

To return to de Certeau's language: we need to abandon top-down *strategies* – not concern ourselves only with legislating for change – and concentrate instead on living *tactically* – allowing our lives to be permeated with an attitude of love for the other that affects all that we do. Love is not a strategy, a top-down plan arranged in a meeting of the board. Love, instead, is a tactic, an attitude to life that pervades all. It is summarised best in Levinas' words: 'The Other has a face, and it is a sacred book in which good is recorded.'[36] Or, as we read earlier, ' "Stop," he seems to be saying to the man hurrying along in the rushing crowd. "There beside you is another person. Meet him . . . Look at the Other's face as he offers it to you. Through this face he shows you yourself: more than that – he brings you closer to God." '[37] Loving, engaging, meeting the other, is intimately connected to meeting them face to face. But this meeting of faces, of eyes, of lips, is not to be romanticised, a danger that critics of Levinas are wary of.

As Christians it should not be difficult to avoid falling for such a romanticised view. This is a faith that asks us to meditate on a face that was beaten beyond recognition, bloodied and smashed by hands and tools. This is a faith that has a kiss as an act of betrayal. In such a faith, any sterilised view of the face of the other as a solely beautiful place which leads us to unity with self and God is quickly sullied and returned to the dirty, complex earth. The other *does* have a face, and it *is* a sacred book in which good is recorded. But it is not an easy read, and the goodness is not always self-evident.

Slavoj Žižek is one strong critic of Levinas, whom he sees as having a too simplistic view of the 'neighbour'. While Levinas is crudely an optimist, who sees the goodness in others as the ground for our love for them, Žižek has a rather darker outlook, taking the Lacanian view that true love for the other springs from the ground of their being *not* perfect.

While all of us want to be in relationship, we all know that we have a fear of engaging the other. Whether this involves loving ourselves properly, or loving God appropriately, or engaging those we live among – noisy neighbours, asylum seekers, travellers – we have all experienced the fear and anxiety that comes with moving outside of our relational comfort zone.

Where does this fear come from? Levinas would argue that we fear connection with the other because we have unresolved fears about the other within *ourselves*. Žižek, on the other hand, would argue that we fear connection with the other because we are wary that the other has unresolved fears within *themselves*. For Levinas, the problem is the enigma *of* the other, for Žižek the problem is the enigma *in* the other: we worry about engagement with our neighbour because we fear their unresolved desires may consume us.

Supporting his argument Žižek quotes Hegel's famous dictum that 'The enigmas of the Ancient Egyptians were also enigmas for the Egyptians themselves.'[38] From Levinas' viewpoint, we are wary of the mysterious Ancient Egyptians because we don't understand them – their actions and language are strange to us, and we would need to overcome the fear within us of this strangeness if we were to engage them. But Žižek – and the line of Hegel and Lacan – would have us reflect that the actions of the Ancient Egyptians were strange *even to themselves*. So if we were to engage them, it would not be simply a case of overcoming *our* fear of their strange ways, but reconciling ourselves to the fact that *they* have not overcome their *own* fear of their *own* strangeness. This principle then reflects back on to us, and our consciousness of the enigmas within each of us too.

Once again, it is useful to meditate on the incarnation in this light. In this thought experiment we can imagine God looking in love on fallen humanity in those last few days and hours before the first Christmas. Did he feel fear about what he was about to undertake? If so, what was the root of that fear? Levinas would locate it within God himself: a concern that he might fail, that these humans that he had created were more of an enigma to him than perhaps he had bargained for. Žižek would locate the fear elsewhere, and I think this is perhaps closer to the truth: God looks down and is concerned less that humans are enigmatic, but more concerned that they are an enigma to themselves. In other words, will they even understand what God is about to do?

God's empathy with us is perhaps thus not grounded in overcoming his internal fear of failure and being able to look at us from a state of fully resolved selfhood, but grounded in accepting what he is going to look like from *our* perspective as conflicted and unresolved selves: 'For Hegel the Incarnation is not a move by means of which God makes himself accessible/visible to humans, but a move by means of which God looks at himself from the (distorting) human perspective.'[39]

As we come to a place where we desire to engage the other we will have to, like God on the cusp of his own incarnation, reflect on the grounds of both our empathy for, and fear of, them. Are we concerned that they won't understand what we are trying to do, or is our fear that they themselves will not understand their own situation? I believe that the truth lies somewhere in the dance between Levinas and Žižek, where they twirl, eye to eye. Levinas leads off: the other has a face, there is goodness within them that we can learn from. Žižek grabs him and spins: but the face of the Other is riddled with enigma and conflict. Levinas draws him close: yes, but look at the other's face as he offers it to you; through it you will see yourself. Žižek throws Levinas and catches him: the sight of the enigma within the other is a mirror on the enigmas within myself. They bow together: and a mirror on those within God too.

Both agree on this: it is only in coming face to face with the other that we begin this dance, this interplay between my conflicts and theirs. To empathise with them I must simultaneously look on them with compassion *and* attempt to see myself from their perspective. The parole officer must seek to understand the released prisoner. They must relinquish their fear and work hard to understand their motivations, to see the humanity and hurt behind the tough façade. This is what Levinas demands. But Žižek would want him or her to go further, and look so closely into the face of this 'other' that they begin to understand how the released prisoner is likely to view *them* in their position as parole officer.

This is what we attempt when we look into the face of the other: not to simply see them, but look deeply enough *to see them seeing us*. In this way I think any attempt to create different poles from Levinas' and Žižek's position would be disingenuous: their two positions are best understood as complimentary. We can begin by affirming Levinas: the other *does* have a face, and it is a sacred book in which good is recorded . . . But we should then also affirm that the text of that sacred book has things not only to say about the other, but about ourselves too. In the robust gaze between ourselves and the other, in the infinite reflections between these pupils, we learn to see them and ourselves in a new light, and hope that they do too. This will be no quick glance. Rather, it will occur only when we give ourselves enough face-to-face time with people, unmediated by screens or other interruptions to our vision.

In his debut feature film *Hunger*, the Turner Prize-winning artist Steve McQueen tackled the subject of IRA prisoner Bobby Sands and his hunger strike. In the central scene of the film Sands sits across a small table from a priest, and, after some initial banter, begins to explain to him what he plans to do – starve himself to death. There follows an intense and highly charged conversation about theology, family, politics and memory that McQueen captures in a single thirteen-minute static shot. The priest learns a great deal about Sands and his internal motivations, but he also learns a lot about how Sands sees him and his theology and his ministry. It is a genuinely powerful piece of cinema and we should be clear where the power comes from: the unblinking gaze of the camera looking in on two people speaking eye to eye about matters of life and death. This conversation could not have happened by telephone. The same words could have been typed into an email exchange or done as a set of wall-to-walls on Facebook, but the power of reciprocated vision, of an eye seeing itself reflected in another eye, would have disappeared.

Our aspiration is to see the other face to face and read the sacred texts that are written there. With its promise of deep connection it seems Face-book was well named, but we must not be fooled into thinking that its groups and campaigns are any substitute for time spent face to face. We need to make sure that we clear proper time in contemplation of this trinity of faces.

I have a face. There are parts of me I want to remain faceless and anonymous – without a name. But if I am to properly see the goodness within me I need not so much to 'deny myself' but *admit* myself to myself – admit what I look like from the perspective of this 'other' within myself. Too often I want to control my public profile, the parts of myself that I can face others seeing, and push down and deny those parts of me that I find ugly or embarrassing or difficult. In fact, as we allow the dappled light of the clearing to warm us, it is out of the compost of these dirty places that riches and growth will be found.

God has a face. There are icons and depictions that I favour, and divine complexities I would rather ignore. But unless I am prepared to seek out these different facets of God, to leave my quarters and pursue my lover, then my faith will dry up and petrify in the stale air of my locked room. It is comforting to imagine myself being watched over by a benevolent, bound-to-me divinity, but I also need to contemplate what it feels like to be watched over by a strange and separate God.

The other has a face. And we must look into it so deeply that we begin to see what the other sees of me, and work out our lives together. There is no personal salvation: I cannot work out my own deliverance from within myself, or theorise my view of God from the comfort of my own home. If I am to experience and know love in any way at all then I need the sacred text of the other.

x X x

Losing our lives

This is the paradox that Jesus engaged with when he said, 'whoever loses his live for my sake will find it.' If I am to find salvation, then I need to forget about my salvation, and go to give everything and serve others. So central does this teaching appear to be to Jesus' message that it is one of only a handful of phrases we find in all four Gospels – and it appears in two of the Gospels more than once. No other saying in the canon of the four Gospels is given more emphasis than this verbal Möbius strip: if I want to save my life I lose it, but if I lose my life, then I save it.

The problem with this paradox is that we appear to be back with Derrida and the 'gift of death': even if I did lay down my life, would there still be a part of me that would be doing so selfishly in order to gain my life back? Reading Jesus' words with Derrida it seems that salvation, like the perfect gift, becomes impossible: no one can lose his or her life without some selfish kernel remaining of wanting to save it, and thus no one is saved. We are caught in a constant bind of personal benefit and sacrifice – our deliverance a gift that is impossible to give and impossible to receive.

As with the impossibility of the cargo-less gift, are we forever stuck, unable to resolve the problem of self-denial and self-preservation? Some have decided that we are, and have given up wrestling with this text. Neutering the most important phrase in the Gospels, they have collapsed the paradox held within it by siding with selfishness. They practise a religion of the self, a prosperous gospel housed in a gated development, dedicated to the service of a domesticated God. From this comfortable bed is conceived fear of difference, mistrust of strangers and a self-righteous faith that leads to fundamentalism. On the surface this fundamentalism seems so right and true. It believes strongly, and prays fiercely for revival. But one wonders if these prayers are perhaps pleas for God to make everyone like us, to turn the other into someone who believes the same things that we do. Realising that there will be wicked and stubborn others who refuse to become like us, we then pray for God to cleanse and purify our land, to banish wickedness and build a new utopia . . . and, horrifically, in Rwanda God appeared to answer.

Since the 1930s many parts of East Africa enjoyed what many people termed a full-scale revival. With centres in Kenya, Tanzania, Rwanda and Uganda, the Christian message spread from a tiny mission station in Gahini, Rwanda, with spectacular speed and in the early 1990s around 90 per cent of Rwandans called themselves Christians. There was heavy emphasis on repentance and morality, and one of the driving forces of the movement was the perceived 'coldness' of the Anglican churches in the region – contrasting with the culturally engaged and 'hot' Pentecostal churches. Major claims have been made for the revival, including that it 'enhanced trans-ethnic integration' and 'gave the believers hope for eternal life [so they] stopped being frightened of death'.[40] One thing it failed to do, however, was improve literacy rates, leaving a population highly dependent on their leaders and the media for instruction.

In 100 days between April and July of 1994, between 800,000 and 1,000,000 Tutsis and Hutu moderates were killed by Hutu

militias. Most of those involved in stirring up the killing, over-
seeing it and carrying it out, were children of the East African
revival. Many Christian leaders were fully complicit in the killing. What possibly could revival have meant if it resulted in this
chronic breakdown between two ethnic groups? Even now maga-
zines like *Christianity Today* would prefer to print reports that
'things are happening!' in Rwanda and that 'this is the result of
prayer and fasting and seeking the face of the Lord – things are
going to explode in the Kingdom of God as we first seek his righteousness', while only giving an obtuse reference to the killing in
the past, saying with alarming ambiguity that 'you can't understand how genocide could have gone on after that revival in the
1930s – [but] it was only an inch deep and a mile wide'.[41]

A salvation that has been gained without putting to death the
self in order to save the other can end up like this, still ready to
take up machetes against my 'Christian brothers' because they are
from another tribe. A revival that has failed to get people to read,
so that they might understand for themselves, rather than being
dependent forever on us and our teaching, is only life sustained
through mouth-to-mouth resuscitation. A body is not revived
until it can breathe and think for itself.

Throughout the continent, the Church's role in Africa has
been traumatic, to say the least. One only need read Thomas
Pakenham's definitive book *The Scramble for Africa* to see that
the auspices of mission were often a paper-thin excuse for exploi-
tation of resources, and that the nature of evangelism was very
heavily biased towards the 'first half of life' approach discussed
earlier.

What the Rwandan tragedy exemplifies for us is the desperate
need we have for a new form of Christian development practice.
It is strategic, top-down, empirical, fundamentalist faith and politics that have left the continent so ravaged. But what is true at this
macro zoom level also holds closer to home. It is the same fallacy
of Christian 'development' at the personal level that has left many
scarred, depressed and angry. Right-wing, prosperity-driven,

fundamentalist Christianity has left a huge political, social, cultural and spiritual fall-out that we see in the resurgence of an equally hard-line New Atheism.

In a sense then this book is simply a plea to see Jesus' summary of the law as a new form of development practice, one that sees the face of the other as its sacred text. It is a practice that is equally concerned with the personal as with the local, the national and international dimensions. Somalia, the Taliban, the tragedy of suicide rates in our provincial towns, the situation in Israel/Palestine, increasing rates of depression, the war in Afghanistan, the moral vacuums exposed by the credit crunch: all of these are issues of *development*. We need to become more mature selves, better able to understand the other both within and without the self. We need to become more mature nations, better able to understand the needs of the international community, and we need to become more mature neighbours, able to see that our destinies are intimately tied up with one another.

Our development practice, based on an immanent God and a utopian ideal, has failed in so many ways. We need to be much wiser. We need a new vision of development that is based on new ideals.

Not seeking permanence, it will hold to a tactic of TAZ, because it is only in the temporary that the spectre of imperialism can be escaped.

Not seeking a profit, it will be wise to the distinctions between what is in the economy of gift, and what is in the economy of trade. But, over all of this, it will be prepared, through music and feasting and festival, to refuse to collapse the paradox of this impossible gift of salvation into a personal transaction based on the self, and will instead seek to explore the mystery of this strange gift through a tactic of love, based on the practice of empathy with the other that begins face to face. This gaze is no saccharine romance. It is an ocular wrestling match, a determined and robust attempt to see the other and see myself through the other's eyes too. What we will see there are paradoxes. As we meet the other face to face we will experience both our separation from them, and our binding to them. As we allow our eyes to search one another, we will see that the grounds of our being and theirs lie in both facticity and transcendence. It is because we are separate that we have the freedom to help. It is because we are bound that we have the obligation to do so. It is because we both have facticity that we cannot deny the facts of our situation. It is because we both experience transcendence that we can have hope of a more peaceful and just world.

One wonders what happened to the teacher who, impressed with what he was hearing, asked Jesus' to summarise the law for him. Jesus' reply was so simple, covering no more than a few dozen words, yet the complexity of unpacking these three simple instructions has continued to challenge us. From ministry to the poor to the birth of hospitals and hospices, from an holistic view of self to struggles for civil liberties and human rights, and with the continuing struggle to incarnate this very carnal God, we have constantly had to re-imagine what love for the other might mean in the context that we find ourselves in.

In the emerging world of virtual presence, global warming, religious intolerance and international terrorism, and with ever-increasing levels of anxiety, depression, relational fracture and social unrest it is vital that this work of re-imagination continues. It will be an emergent, complex and adaptive re-imagination that will need to be done in each local context by each local body. I cannot mow you down with a list of bullet points, a step-by-step programme for you to follow in your area. But nor can I do nothing and so, as we turn to our final section, I want to outline some examples from my own situation of how this new development practice might look in one particular context, the one in which I find myself.

PART FOUR

LOVING THE OTHER IN PRAXIS

Spirituality is not to be learned in flight from the world, by fleeing from things to a place of solitude; rather we must learn to maintain an inner solitude regardless of where we are or whom we are with. We must learn to penetrate things, and find God there.[1]

Meister Eckhart

Eckhart knew that spirituality – healthy human development by another name – is not to be found by running away from the world to our own personal clearing. Rather, we must learn to take the clearing with us, to find that inner desert and take it out in search of the other. For it is in that pursuit that we will find fulfilment. Not our *own* fulfilment, because anyone who tries to find their own life will lose it, but our fulfilment together.

This is the radical message of the incarnation: do whatever it takes to go in search of the Other, because it was only in that process of incarnation, of stepping into the perspective of the Other, that God opened up the process of reconciliation – between God and us, and God and Godself.

x X x

Engaging the other within the self

Turning off – the radio-silent self

If the mantra of the emancipated 1960s was 'Turn on, tune in, drop out', then perhaps our mantra for a re-emancipation of the self should begin with turning *off*. At the core of our personal spiritual/developmental practice must be an affirmation of ourselves as separate and bound beings. We need to pursue personal Temporary Autonomous Zones: spaces where we can rediscover the marvellous and experience freedom from the systems that we spend so much time servicing.

Let me emphasise again: I am not anti-technology. I do, however, share concerns with others that the balance between our useful co-operation with digital technology and unhealthy dependence on it is in danger of tipping the wrong way. Jamais Cascio, a senior fellow at the Institute for Ethics and Emerging Technologies, is optimistic about the future of a constantly connected world, and sees that the 'technology-induced Attention Deficit Disorder that's associated with this new world may be a short-term problem'.[2] Our close interaction with the web will, in his view augment our intelligence. This is probably irrefutable: greater and freer access to information will increase our knowledge. What is less certain is whether it will improve our wisdom, or the quality of our relationships.

Susan Greenfield, Professor of Synaptic Pharmacology at Oxford University recently remarked that:

> My worry is when anyone does anything in excess. If you're living a fulfilled life in 3 dimensions, then occasionally going into 2 dimensions will be fine. The brain is very good at what it rehearses. The more you rehearse something, the better you are at it, and if you don't rehearse it, you won't be good at it. So if, because you're communicating with 900 'friends' every day, you don't rehearse the normal, complex, highly challenging interaction of face-to-face conversation where you're going on tone of voice, body language or perhaps picking up on pheromones, then you won't be good at it, you'll find it quite stressful, which means you'll do it less because you'll tend to do the thing that you enjoy most, so it'll be a vicious circle.[3]

If we are to ensure that our increased knowledge is partnered with improved relationships then part of our healthy practice will be a commitment to making sure that we do spend time offline and do leave time for face-to-face conversation. More than that though, we need to give time to silence. Not simply the silence of no conversation or audible noise, but radio silence too: turning off our wireless devices and committing to simply being in the physically present space we are in, rather than being carried off by the immediate demands of text messages, emails and tweets. In a world of virtual presence, it is no longer enough for spiritual development to have physical solitude. Digital solitude is also something that now needs to be pursued, not that we are seeking to reject technology – just as physical solitude is not about a rejection of community – but that we are fasting from it in order to make our appetite for it a healthy one.

The Jewish principle of Sabbath has fallen into absurdity in many ways – as highlighted by the recent case of a Jewish couple suing their landlord, who had installed motion-sensing lighting on the stairs outside their apartment.[4] Triggering these automatic lights was defined as work under Sabbath law, so his attempt at environmentalism was, according to the case they filed, causing them to sin. However ridiculous some of these extreme cases have become, and the technology that has been developed to get round them, the Sabbath principle is perhaps one that is demanding a fresh look. Previous 'Keep Sunday Special' campaigns have focused on retail opening hours, with right concerns that all workers are given common recreation time to spend together with their families, but perhaps now the emphasis needs to change. The exact time of the week is unimportant, but, like those ancient Jewish farmers, what we need is a regular time when we can down tools and remind ourselves of our separation from them and the earth.

Work, and all the associated business of our lives, can be a way of simply avoiding the silence that comes with Sabbath. Church services too, these supposed shared moments of Sabbath, can seem deliberately contrived to eliminate all silence. Why? What are we afraid of? To paraphrase Mark Edmondson, perhaps we are afraid of meeting our 'great Antagonist'. The fear of silence is loneliness, and loneliness is not a fear of being alone, but a fear of whom we are with when we *are* alone.

This was the personal TAZ that Jesus deliberately stepped into in the wilderness. Its temporal nature was important: silence is not to be elevated as a permanent goal, but its autonomy was vital too. Jesus fasted and prayed as a conscious movement into *autos nomos*: 'self law'. He knew that he would not face his demons as he continued in hard carpentry. In his hunger and temptation he lived fully in the heat of the paradox of separation and binding. He was bound to the earth, needing to feed from it to sustain his life, but his act of fasting was a statement of autonomous separation too.

Part of a healthy development practice will be to take diversions into these wilderness spaces on a regular basis. Short moments, longer stretches, daily, weekly, monthly or annually – the details will emerge in your local context, but the principle is an important one: seek regular silence.

Fruit

I want to change the fruits of my labours:
When someone says 'Apple',
I don't want to know
white plastic and titanium,
But England's Coxes,
heavy hung in dappled orchards.

When someone says 'Orange',
I don't want to know
free minutes or latest upgrades.
I want to think citrus thoughts;
the tang and appeal of slowly peeling skin.

And when someone says 'Blackberry',
I don't want to think
virtual thoughts of emails, deadlines,
documents, settings, schedules,
coverage and battery life.
I want, instead, my tongue
to rush with sweet sensation:
A bowl of fruits shared among friends.
A rug.
Open space.
Blue sky.

Walking – the still self

For those who find the movement into silence and stillness too much, walking may be a good solution. Get off the bus a couple of stops early, walk your neighbourhood in the early evening, or get out to a park or into countryside. In conversation with the keen walker and psychogeographer Will Self, Geoff Nicholson notes that:

> I agree with [Will] about the disembodied, meditative aspect of walking. I often find, especially if I'm walking a long way, that I start out very thoughtful and attentive, observing things, having lofty thoughts, making sentences in my head, but then after a few hours I've stopped all that. I'm just putting one foot in front of the other, just walking.[5]

He goes on to quote the prolific walker Sebastian Snow, who trekked the entire length of South America: 'By some transcendental process, I seemed to take on the characteristics of a Shire [horse], my head lowered, resolute, I just plunked one foot in front of t'other, mentally munching nothingness.'

This is one of the delights of walking: beyond the thoughts that race and the concerns about destination and time comes the state of 'mentally munching nothingness' – a wonderful description of the sense of transcendent separation from the earth, even while becoming so bound to it in our boots.

I am writing this late at night in a tent in the Peak District, and have enjoyed some wonderful walking today in sun and rain through some wonderful countryside. Walking through 'nature' is good for the soul, and reminds us of our ancient connections with the earth and thus with our creator. But the God we meet in these wild walks is mostly the God of the wild nature we come across; mountains tell us simple truths of God's sublime power, lakes and rivers of God's care. When we are not mentally munching nothingness the message of the hills is straightforward: I exist, I care about you, there are bigger things in the world.

Intentional walking in the city is far less common, but equally rewarding. In fact, an urban walk can be even more rewarding than a hike in the hills simply because of the surprises it can throw up. Much of the walking we do in the city is functional: we need to get from A to B and do so with our heads down, our ears filled with tunes and our senses tuned out to those making their way around us. To walk intentionally is paradoxically to walk with none of these functional intentions. It is simply to decide to walk without purpose. To simply step out and enjoy what the city places before us.

The messages we get on these urban walks are much more complex. As we open our eyes to the architecture, to the history of stones quarried and formed and piled high, we begin to appreciate the city as living testament to divine-human cooperation. This can be an amazingly energising experience – our eyes opened to the New Jerusalem hints of the communality and shared public space that our cities can offer. But it can also be a cathartic and therapeutic experience too. If flying from London to New York, Will Self makes a point of walking to the airport outside London (about twenty-five miles, or a good day's hike), flying, then walking to wherever he is staying at the other end. Why? To overcome the distance-collapsing, time-warping and culture-mashing effects of intercontinental travel. The novelist Iain Sinclair has done many intentional walks through London, but is perhaps best known for attempting to exorcise the spirit of Margaret Thatcher by walking anti-clockwise around the acoustic-footprint of the M25 in *London Orbital*. This is hiking as spiritual practice, following in the footsteps of Jesus, centring the self and reawakening our humanity.

Meditating – the disturbed self

To walk is to take time in the physical present, and I am committed to doing more of it. Beyond that though, I want also to begin to engage in the ancient practice of meditation. (I am thankful for the work my sister has done in this area, modelling a Christian meditative practice that takes seriously the experience of other faith traditions.)

The Benedictine monk John Main is widely thought of as one of the pioneers of Christian meditation. In 1954 he was in Kuala Lumpur with the British Colonial Service where he met a Hindu swami, who taught him the principle of meditation using a mantra. Main later returned to Dublin and then joined the Benedictines in London, where he introduced meditation using a Christian mantra and also explored the connections between what he had begun to practise and the writings of John Cassian, one of the early Desert Fathers. Having worried that the practice would be complex, I have been relieved to discover that the essence of Main's (and others) teaching on meditation is so profoundly simple that I can repeat it here in full:

> Sit down. Sit still and upright. Close your eyes lightly. Sit relaxed but alert. Silently, interiorly begin to say a single word.

> We recommend the prayer-phrase Maranatha. Recite it as four syllables of equal length. Listen to it as you say it, gently but continuously.

> Do not think or imagine anything spiritual or otherwise. If thoughts and images come, these are a distraction at the time of meditation, so keep returning to simply saying the word.

> Meditate each morning and evening for between 20 and 30 minutes.[6]

Don't try to think about anything, but don't be worried when thoughts come and disturb you. Simply put them aside and return to the mantra. In this way we are, for a short time, attempting a single-minded point of attention, for what we give our attention to is what we love. Like any activity, practice will be key, and a determination not to give up quickly when it becomes hard. Thomas Merton in his *Thoughts in Solitude* makes it clear that there will be difficulties: 'One cannot enter then into meditation, in this sense, without a kind of inner upheaval. By upheaval I do not mean a disturbance, but a breaking out of routine, a liberation of the heart from the cares and preoccupation of one's daily business.'[7]

As Merton explored towards the end of his life, the Buddhist tradition has also had an impact on Christian meditation. For a Buddhist, the goal is to 'walk the middle way between attraction and aversion' and thus experience 'total presence'. The Buddha discovered that to really embody this it was not enough to simply 'be' in the present moment, but that he had to move beyond his own experience into 'oneness'. But beyond oneness he perceived an even more fundamental reality, an energetic disruption, what the Desert Fathers came to name as a force beyond unity, a 'holy dissatisfaction'.

While meditation is about a sense of inner peace, it is not necessarily about achieving *total* equilibrium within the self. Within the practice is a desire to see beyond surface ideas of unity, and to engage with the disruption and dissatisfaction that lies beneath. I am aware that people, like myself, come to meditation because they sense a need to engage in something that might help 'defrag' the self, but the trajectory of it is perhaps better seen as aiming to go through that defragmentation, and then begin to see the holy dissatisfaction beyond it. Meditation can be seen as one way of exploring a 'daily Sabbath'. It is not an escape from the disruptions of life, it *is* a disruption that aims to reconfigure the whole of life.

While travelling through Derbyshire recently, I came across an advertisement for a shopping centre that read:

Sunday is a Day for ~~Rest~~ Shopping

We can read this two ways: either rest is being replaced by shopping, or equated to shopping. The idea of Sabbath rest is not being rejected, it is being co-opted. The message of the advertisement is that recreation has to be achieved – that is not under negotiation – but this Sabbath rest is achieved through consumption. We are recharged, are re-envisioned and re-made by drawing in resources from without, by spending and expending. 'Having has replaced Being.'[8]

Meditation stands in opposition to this and in a world where shopping is relaxation, it perhaps becomes the most radical gesture. In meditation the aim is to do nothing, to communicate with no one, to spend nothing. Meditation is free. It consumes nothing except the time that it takes, and is thus seen by the consumer-capitalist hegemony as utterly wasteful. In the time of meditation we are out of reach. Our phones will not be answered, our emails not read, our social networks not updated. Flying in the face of Facebook, during meditation *we have no status*. There is nothing to report other than I AM. This is the personal TAZ, a place set aside for a short while where we allow something marvellous to penetrate. Combined with a commitment to action (which ensures we do not fall into the trap Žižek identifies of meditation becoming a fetish that allows us to peacefully co-exist in a corrupt and violent society) it is an act of personal piracy: a stealing back of time, a redistribution of resources, an agitation to the authorities and map-makers and empirical forces who can only see a lack of useful work, a wasting of time, a dangerous heresy. It is not the ethereal, escapist practice of those who want a perfect view of the self, but the disturbing, interrupting practice of those who refuse to believe the *comfort, comfort* voices of the system.

Playing – the challenged self

Tough critics might argue that my football playing is rather too like meditation: I do very little of use! Perhaps you are talented in this area; I am not – and that is the point. Playing football has become one very simple way in which I have begun to move beyond a too-comfortable view of the self.

For the majority of my waking hours I am engaged in activities at which I succeed. I am a good teacher. I am a reliable father. I can cook. People seem to appreciate what I write. Filling my days with things that I feel confident about and competent in is a sure-fire way to give me a distorted view of my Self: I am successful. I am good. I am top of the pile.

So, stepping onto a football pitch is, for me, a brilliant way of reminding myself that other people are far better at things than I am. I am not *so* awful that my participation spoils the game for the other players – that would be the height of arrogance. But I am sufficiently worse to be picked last, to be responsible for the opposition scoring on regular occasions, and for people to be pleasantly surprised when I score.

As it turns out, playing football is, for me, rather like meditation. It is a disruption, a challenge to the easy equilibrium of the rest of my life. I play because I love it – not for some spiritual flagellation – but having something regular in my week where I see my own failings clearly, and yet remain accepted by the group I play with, has become important to me.

I think this is connected with Edmundson's plea for us not to run away from facing our antagonists. In the digital lives that we are able to assemble for ourselves – with focused news feeds and carefully selected blogs listed on our readers – it is difficult to see where the antagonisms and challenges are going to come from. It ought to be part of our practice to introduce a feed from a blogger we profoundly disagree with, or occasionally buy a newspaper that we don't connect so well with, and read all of it.

In very simple ways like this we can challenge the sterilised and obvious facticity of what we like and who we listen to, and thus reinvigorate the paradoxical tension of who we are. Perhaps this is why Jesus dined with tax collectors, spoke with Samaritan women and touched lepers: not simply because it spoke of radical acceptance, but because it disturbed his sense of comfort too, and re-energised not just the public debate about religion, but his private negotiation of the self.

This is a vital point for us to appreciate: the self is not to be mined into ever deeper and darker depths, in some search for profound unity. This is where I would want to disassociate from monastic practice that is not connected to the real world, and is focused purely on a solitary work of refining and purifying the self. In my readings of Thomas Merton I find myself thinking that this was a tension he experienced profoundly; he wanted still to be in the jazz clubs, to be meeting 'real' people – and his latter forays back into that scene, seen as sinful lapses, were actually wonderful rediscoveries of parts of himself that he had suppressed. To attempt to engage the other within the self is to simultaneously seek a more mature self, and admit that it is only in conjunction with external disturbances that this can occur.

So via Merton we return to Eckhart: this is not a selfish journey of introspection; there is no genuine spirituality to be found there. Rather, it is belief that temporary, autonomous moments spent in the silence of the clearing can help us appreciate better the centrality of disturbance to our development. We withdraw from others for a moment to help us better appreciate the other.

In a restatement of Eckhart, Žižek puts it like this: 'The central feature of the Judeo-Christian tradition is that man's encounter with divinity is not the result of withdrawal into the depths of my inner Self and the ensuing realization of the identity of the core of my Self and the core of Divinity.'[9] We do not find our deep connection with God by mining deep inside of our self. Instead, and he posits this as an argument for the intimate link between Judaism and psychoanalysis, 'the focus is on the traumatic encounter with the abyss of the desiring Other'.

This is surely Buddha's disruption, the radical disturbance of meditation and the Desert Fathers' 'holy dissatisfaction' by another name. It is in the practices that allow us a clearer reflection on the self that we find that there are deep disturbances and abysses: and it is within these that we begin to experience connection with God. These are strange places to explore, for sure. So we rightly gather with others who have been disturbed by this abyss and try to walk and learn together. So it is to the Other within our faith that we now turn.

Engaging the Other within our faith

As we 'go in search of the Other' we will need to reflect on our personal practices, the spiritual disciplines if you will, that will lead us towards healthy development of the self – or, in more modern terms, greater integration between the selves that are part of the constant negotiation of who we are. This is our response to Jesus' implicit command to love ourselves as part of his summary of the law, his précis of a life centred on integrated human development.

This command to love ourselves was taken as given; Jesus' command to love God was the first explicit point in response to being asked what the most important commandment was. How then can we better love God, better engage together this 'Other' that disturbs us, leads us, hides from us and inspires us?

In my view our corporate Christian practice has tended to answer this by institutionalising God. Though Jesus had a temporal physical ministry and reserved his heaviest criticism for those who saddled believers with heavy loads of religion, the Church has continued to pursue a model based on permanent structures and observance of partisan creeds. I sincerely believe that if we are to be faithful to Christ's command to love God then we need a new corporate practice.

Church as TAZ

Against the model of church as a permanent structure, offering a familiar liturgical rhythm of worship which appears to take as its inspiration the parable of the persistent widow – grinding down God into submission through constant nagging – I have tried to offer a vision of corporate Christian life inspired by the theory of Temporary Autonomous Zones.

The TAZ is 'like an uprising which does not engage directly with the State, a guerrilla operation which liberates an area (of land, of time, of imagination) and then dissolves itself to re-form elsewhere/elsewhen, before the State can crush it'.[10] It 'envisions an intensification of everyday life, or as the Surrealists might have said, life's penetration by the Marvellous'.[11]

These penetrations are temporary for good reason. First, it is the only way to avoid the perils of utopian visions, which lead to exclusion or violation. Second, all acts of worship are essentially acts of spiritual cartography. Given that we are destined to see through a glass darkly, our gatherings can only be a representation of a greater reality that we hope for. Our liturgies, our services, our songs, our multimedia offerings are no more than maps of a territory that we have faith we will one day walk in person. We scribble their contours and note down symbols, plotting our bearings and smoothing the folds. But the permanent danger of our institutions is to begin to confuse the map for reality, and worship our particular representation as physically 'true'.

As any walker or driver will tell you, maps are dead documents as soon as they are printed. (They are bound to be: the most up-to-date and accurate map imaginable would have to represent itself as soon as it was created, which it obviously cannot do until the created thing is present to be represented.) This doesn't render maps useless, but it does mean that, unless we are prepared to dispense with them and rework them on a regular basis, we are destined to view the world through the eyes of an interesting historic document, but one which bears little relation to the ground it purports to represent.

This was precisely the reason why, after ten years, we decided to put the public face of Vaux, the community I helped establish, to the sword. To many people on the outside it seemed like a strange decision: what we were doing was still 'successful'. But for those of us on the inside, we knew that the maps that we were using were becoming increasingly dysfunctional and unrepresentative. We had created a set of practices to fit the topology of our faith, but the ground had now changed. We could either soldier on – with the likely result that someone would get hurt or burn out – or decide that the maps had to go. 'You can't stop!' was one message we had from people outside of Vaux who had never actually been; but that they took encouragement from the fact that something like what we did existed, despite never actually coming themselves, was simply not reason enough to continue. We made the decision, met twice more – once for a public 'burning of the maps', and once more for a wake where we celebrated the life that had been – and that was it. We left the building.

Of course, the fantastic hope of the Christian faith is that that is *never* it. Our story is based on the death and resurrection of Christ – yet we appear so afraid to ever allow things to die. What I have always been hugely proud of in Vaux was the courage that people showed to go through with this death. I feel that it was a timely one, and that if we had continued with public expressions then the imperfections in our relationships would have grown to irreparable fissures. That never happened, and we are all still in very regular contact, looking for what the next TAZ might be.

I strongly believe that while the Church has an eternal dimension, our manifestations of church should retain a deliberately temporal one. While maintaining healthy networked relationships with fellow-believers, the public expressions of our faith will emerge and spring up in marvellous ways to temporarily liberate a space or time, but will then disappear before they can petrify and harden.

Transformance art

In many ways taking the baton from Vaux, the Belfast-based group Ikon, co-founded by my good friend Pete Rollins, is modelling some of the key aspects of church as TAZ. Pete would

describe the public aspects of their main services as 'transformance art'. These gatherings are focused on the idea of conversion,
of funding and precipitating substantial change in people over
and above intellectual and theological re-imagination. It is a
full reconfiguration of the social self that concerns them, and
the transformance art at an Ikon gathering attempts to achieve
this through multi-sensory provocation. As Pete has set out in
his books, Ikon's gatherings set out to mimic revelation. The
moment of revelation, as experienced by Paul for example,
can often be a moment of blindness, of incomprehension and
bedazzlement. Revelation is not simply about coming to deeper
understanding – although this may be an end result of it – it is
about opening oneself up to mystery, and to the possibility of
transformation.

Curating spaces within which this can happen is not a straightforward task like planning a traditional service. In a lengthy email
exchange with Jonny Baker, who helps lead the Grace community in London, we discussed some of the moments he had found
particularly powerful at gatherings Vaux had curated. My view
on these stand-out moments is that they are by their very nature
unpredictable, but that they can perhaps be thought about within
the axes of facticity and transcendence.

In one example that Baker raised, we had created a very large-
scale map of London that covered around thirty square feet of the
floor. We asked people to take pens and draw some of the journeys around London that they had made during that week. As
they finished, we switched the light in the space to UV, at which
point it became apparent that the pens were UV sensitive, and
London began to glow with the collected journeys of those gathered. 'This is where Christ has been this week' was all that was
said.

The power of that moment was unpredictable, but I believe
that part of it came from bringing together something very
tactile and physical – the facticity of drawing a journey on a piece
of paper – with a moment whereby that was then transcended

and transformed in an unexpected way. Too often, just as we might live in 'bad faith', we worship in bad faith too, collapsing this vital paradox of facticity and transcendence into one at the expense of the other. Our gatherings can be simply boring communications of information, well-rehearsed lines stating well-worn beliefs. Alternatively, they can be little-understood rituals where we stand as mere spectators, unable to work out what is going on, or why.

What Ikon does so well, and what churches taking TAZ seriously should aim at, is walking this fine line between these two states. It is thus within the paradoxes of what they curate that transformation can occur. These transformance art events are temporal by nature: they exist for a short time – usually just one hour – in a specific location, and then disappear without trace once finished. Ikon happens in a bar in Belfast. Go to that bar now and you will not 'find' Ikon. Go on the evening of the event and you will find a space reconfigured for a short time only, penetrated by something marvellous.

Rollins is very frank about the successes and failures of Ikon, and about the fact that circumstance has often forced them to consider their ideologies as much as theology has. Given the chance to have had a bespoke building and facilities, it may be that they would have taken it, but retrospectively he is very glad that they have never had the chance to do so. Now the fact that they remain 'homeless' and transient – they have used a number of different bars for their gatherings over the years – is central to their ideology. This is a radically different model to that of the mega-church, which wants to create 'facts on the ground' with imposing physical structures and impressive facilities. Church as TAZ then is taking the model of the tabernacle rather than the temple: a temporary, portable structure that claims whatever ground it covers as holy.

Ikon, as with many other similar communities, is taking the idea of TAZ seriously because, as the poet R. S. Thomas has described in 'The Empty Church', the permanent temple has become a stony trap in which belief ossifies and transformation becomes increasingly unlikely.

The counter-argument is that it is only within permanent structures that community can prosper and that the needy can be cared for. I want to analyse this in more depth in general terms later, but Ikon's view is simple: *we don't care about you*. There are no formal pastoral support structures, no teams of carers. And yet, people do experience welcome and care. What Ikon are modelling is a relational network where people are clear about the expectations that they can have of it. In Rollins' view, too many people leave church because they feel that the church said 'we care about you', and what they experienced was something very different from that.

In many churches the basic principle of Christian hospitality has been professionalised into a well-run ministry. There are welcoming teams and regular church lunches and ministries to the poor. While these are obviously commendable, the danger of them is that they create a dynamic among the rest of the congregation that 'care for the other has been taken care of' – and thus people end up abdicating their responsibilities to care for one another. So by making it clear that Ikon *doesn't* care, that there are no ministries or structures that are going to pick this stuff up, ground is cleared for people to evolve caring relationships and to take responsibility for those around them in *ad hoc* ways.[12]

In this sense, groups like Ikon are modelling a faith that is again paradoxical, treading a fine line between separation from one another, and binding to one another. No one has responsibility for care within Ikon, which means that everybody does. Thus, in their art and their relationships, Ikon is living out the separate-and-bound idea of God. God is both accessible and inaccessible, to be understood but never understood.

Returning to a festive religion

The key principle of TAZ, as seen by Hakim Bey and the anarchists and situationists who took the idea to heart, is one of

liberation. With an end goal of a greater, more permanent liberation in mind – of people and of thought – TAZ seeks a temporary
liberation of a physical space or timeframe, the idea being that
simply tasting this new order will lead to it being born at some
later date.

This is very close to the ancient idea of a festival ('carnival' in
Bakhtin's language) in which the usual rules of life are temporarily suspended. We might not wash for a few days; we might eat
strange foods and totally change our sleeping habits. Importantly,
we also meet new people, people we would not normally spend
time with. For a short time, the game changes.

As previously mentioned, I can think of no place where I have
experienced this more profoundly than at the Christian arts festival
Greenbelt. For four days a horse-racing venue in the South-West of
England is temporarily 'liberated' and transformed. Twenty thousand people from the entire spectrum of belief – from evangelical
Christian to atheist to Muslim to Pentecostal to Hindu – populate this new space with music, art, theatre, talks, debates, eating
and drinking. Gently, very gently, people from different traditions
are brought together, and eat and dance and talk together, and
begin to realise that the hard positions they had held for so long
are beginning to melt as they make face-to-face contact with the
other.

Again, the temporal nature of Greenbelt is so important. It would be terrible to have to live in those conditions
for anything other than a few days. Tents are packed closely
together and sanitary facilities are barely adequate. The site
functions perfectly well for four days, but within two weeks
it would doubtless look like a refugee camp, with squabbles
breaking out over resources and space, and illness becoming a
problem. However, the temporary nature and the dirt actually
go hand in hand.

One could imagine holding Greenbelt (or Poland's Slot festival) in a large convention centre: the same people could attend
and the same programme could be created. The same food could

be served and the same clothes worn, but I would argue that the same spirit would not permeate the event. The dirt is central to the spirit of temporary liberation. It is a physical manifestation of a deeper reality: the carnival is a transgressive place, where the normal laws and purity rituals are suspended. It is within these dirty, festive spaces that our boundaries become softer and we become more open to engaging the other in a way that simply would not happen in a clinical, air-conditioned hall.

If the Church, so riven with talk of splits and posturing, is to once again be a place of welcome, of genuine hospitality – a place that models the radical acceptance of God – then I strongly believe that it needs to accept that it is going to be a transgressive place, a place of carnival.

These TAZ spaces are spaces 'in good faith'. They remain located in the same recognisable physical location that we recognise – it is clear that Greenbelt *is* held in a racecourse – but the facticity of these locations is coupled with a transcendent axis too.

The transformation of these geographies into new dimensions permits other movements too. In the upside-down world of the carnival, when rules are being broken and boundaries crossed, we feel far more open to meeting the other. Because *all* are strangers in this new space our natural reserve is reduced and we feel better able to share with one another without fear of power imbalance.

Beyond the large annual festivals like Greenbelt and Slot, our Christian practice should be hallmarked by festivity, by carnival. Rather than putting on evangelistic events at which the gospel will be *explained* in careful language – as if we are trying to convince people of a scientific theory – we should be organising carnival events in which the different world order of the gospel is being *lived out*.

The church's calendar is full of such festival opportunities, but most are neutered by programmes of well-worn liturgy. Why are we missing these opportunities? Christmas is pure carnival: the incarnation, impoverished shepherds and foreign astrologers chosen above faithful priests and established monarchs. Easter is outrageous theatre: a man is brutally betrayed and murdered by an oppressive regime, but mysteriously escapes the clutches of their stone tomb and twenty-four-hour surveillance to appear alive again. Pentecost, Ascension, Lent – throughout the year we have moments with the potential to be infected by the carnival TAZ spirit, to offer a temporary intensification of everyday life, a liberation from the day-to-day, something marvellously counter-cultural where tricksters can begin to play and, in the momentary suspension of the normal rules, we can meet the other and learn from them.

These well-known Christian festivals are key moments of focus, but this TAZ approach to corporate Christian life is equally applicable day by day. Should not our weekly Sabbath be a time of carnival? Rather than a dragging day of slaving through a church service or two, and cocooning ourselves in our comfortable families or church groups, shouldn't we be looking for one day in the week when we celebrate inclusion and festivity? Rather than campaign for shops to be closed and ferries not to run, should we not be modelling ourselves a day of such freedom from the shackles of rampant consumerism that no one visits the shops anyway?

This is piratical Christianity – existing in the spaces outside of the maps that the ruling powers make, bursting through in surprising places to take temporary hold of some space or time. Like Jesus' own ministry – erupting with miracles and healing and encounters with lepers and outcasts – it will be berated as heresy by those in authority. But for those brave enough to join up, it will be a life of high adventure whose highest goal is to see orthodoxy revitalised by this carnival of dirt.

Moreover though, it is within these carnival spaces, where we meet the other as we celebrate our life transformed by the Other, that we will be urged to move out from the comforts of our own situations and empathise with those beyond our faith and experience. It is vital that we engage in spiritual practices that will help us towards a better understanding of the self. It is vital that in our corporate Christian practice we are modelling the life and work of a God who is both separate and bound, who is a God of festivity and carnival. But beyond both of these, it is also vital that we move out beyond our churches to engage the other in our cities, in our politics and wherever we find injustice. As Karl Barth famously noted in his *Church Dogmatics*, 'No praise of God is serious, or can be taken seriously, if it is apart from or in addition to the commandment: "*Thou shalt love thy neighbour as thyself.*" '[13] And so, having journeyed through what it might mean to love ourselves and to love God, we come finally to the practicalities of loving our neighbour.

Engaging the other within our communities

Becoming generous churches: the food pantry

Our faith communities' interactions with the communities that host them should be hallmarked by generosity. In his Reith Lectures, given at the invitation of the BBC in June 2009, the political philosopher Michael Sandel set out a vision for 'a new politics of the common good'. One of the key themes that cropped up repeatedly as he covered ground such as genetics, market economics and politics was that in this age when 'market triumphalism' is over, it will be generosity towards one another that should define our public life.

Sandel uses some interesting examples to make his point. A study done in Israel recently examined what happened when a children's nursery began fining parents if they picked their children up late. Surprisingly, late pick-ups actually increased. Why? Because the introduction of money removed any relational or empathetic obligation the parents may have felt to get to the nursery on time at the end of each day. It's fine if we're late: we'll just pay.

Work has also been done researching the best way to get people to give blood. Market economics would have us believe that introducing a payment for the blood you give would encourage people to give more. It doesn't. A pay-for-blood system (as used in the US) harvests not only *less* blood, but less *usable* healthy blood than a blood-as-gift system (as used in the UK).

Finally, Sandel outlines his philosophical opposition to the 'carbon credits' schemes that have been part of the conditions for the US joining any global carbon emission reduction scheme. His point is that the introduction of a market in carbon simply allows the rich to pay for their pollution. They see the money involved not as a fine, but as a charge and thus their empathy towards the root of the issue – good stewardship of the earth – is diminished. Companies should *want* to reduce their carbon footprints, and be shamed into doing so if they don't. A carbon market may prevent this relational impetus from functioning properly.

In other words, market economics have their place, but often the market gets into places it simply shouldn't be, and the results can be disastrous – not only to the environment, but to our personal wellbeing too.

The *Observer* magazine recently ran a piece entitled 'Welcome to the Age of Exhaustion', that outlined just how ill and anxious our permanent submersion in a culture of work and profitable economic activity can make us.[14] Frank Lipman, a New York doctor, is quoted as having seen hundreds of patients suffering from chronic fatigue and anxiety, and makes a radical diagnosis of their condition: they are 'spent'. He is spot on. In a world of ubiquitous consumer ideologies, what better way to describe those who cannot compete any more? They are spent people, with no more in the bank. They are poor in spirit, and in desperate need of blessing.

This is 'the other' within our community: it is our neighbour who is poor, our fellow citizens who are spent. Poverty is a global problem which will require our generous hospitality if it is to be solved, but we must have as rich and broad a view of poverty as

Jesus himself did, seeing the aching poverty in the wealthy tax collector and the empty religion of the Pharisees as well as the hungry mouths of the crowds. His solution was not a call for markets to be dismantled ('Give to Caesar what is Caesar's . . .') but for them to be removed from the places where generosity should be the governing economic – as he displayed in his 'cleansing of the temple'.

In our attempts to develop a healthy sense of self and a robust view of the otherness within God, we are doing no more than our own act of clearing in order that we can better offer hospitality to our neighbours. One hardly need look very far to see that such a 'new politics of the common good' is desperately needed. Violent crime among teenagers is increasing, stress-related illness continues to rise, relationships are under more and more pressure, nationalism is on the rise again in Europe with aggression against immigrants and asylum seekers a continuing problem, fundamentalist believers are increasingly using violent techniques to try to get their voices heard and opinions adopted, and the warning signs over major conflicts over natural resources in an increasingly unpredictable global climate are becoming ever stronger while ranks of wealthy Christians line up in huge churches begging for 'more, Lord'.

From the masculine side we have already seen the narrative archetype of the hero needing to become the heir. From the feminine perspective, if the Church is the 'Bride of Christ' I imagine Jesus is getting rather frustrated by his betrothed's behaviour. Two thousand years you have been calling yourself my bride! All this singing and swooning and calling for greater intimacy with me! When will you stop being the passive *bride* and start doing your work as *mother* to this poor earth?!

As we look at some examples of how people have worked this out in practice, we need to hold these principles in mind: the Church acting to serve the other is the Church wanting to move from the passive role of bride to the active role of parent, and, as we saw in Sandel's earlier thoughts on parenting, being 'open to the unbidden'. When 90 per cent of those in the criminal justice system in the UK are known to have had an identified conduct disorder as a child, it is clear that parenting is a hugely important area within which the church needs to offer support. This is not about patronising those around us, for, as we saw with the example of the feast at which the host lifts the bread to heaven in order to be a corecipient of the generous gift of food, all of us are interdependent and require one another if we are to find a proper sense of ourselves, our faith and our communities. This is about the Church returning to a radical sense of being hospitable, of living within the gift and modelling that generous mindset to a poor world through the carnival spirit of the TAZ.

Perhaps the best example of this that I have come across is the Food Pantry run by Sara Miles out of St Gregory of Nyssa Church in San Francisco. Each week they collect around five tonnes of fresh groceries – much of it 'misfit' food that supermarkets won't take because it doesn't look perfect – and distribute it to around 500 families who come to the church each Friday. The queues of people waiting to get food can stretch for two blocks, but the volunteers in the church are careful to only let a few in at a time so that people won't feel rushed or insignificant. The goal is to treat everyone with dignity and this means that, though things take a little longer, it's 'more like a celebration than a handout'.[15]

The Food Pantry is a generous TAZ space where each week, for a short time, something marvellous happens. People are offered food without exception. No 'purity checks' are done, no questionnaires are filled in and no means testing takes place. Whoever walks in the door is offered good food – mostly by volunteers who come to help because they received help in the past. Food for these volunteers is cooked up by the priest, Paul Fromont, who sees this as an essential part of his role: feeding people. And so, through this simple act of generosity, the poor, the homeless, the marginalised, the old, the crippled, the strange, the foreign, the parent-less are all brought through the doors of the church to receive food from the same altar that serves bread and wine on a Sunday. Are these not the same people that Jesus sat and ate with? By sharing food with them he was engaging them in a marvellous feast – a temporary moment of inclusion in a world of exhausting alienation. It is to these generous encounters that we should commit ourselves.

Just a thought

The polymath René Descartes,
described life at its thoughtful heart:
'je pense donc je suis' –
it's *thinking* makes me –
was a 'sophical work of art.

But the converse of what he had said
brings an interesting thought to my head:
when they rage in their cars,
elbow people in bars
can it be that the *thoughtless* are *dead*?

Becoming communities of encounter: street pastors and public houses

In an article for the British politics and arts magazine *Prospect* David Lammy, a Member of Parliament for the diverse London constituency of Tottenham, draws on research that shows that simply 'increasing the level of contact between different groups is enough to generate more favourable relationships between them'.[16]

He continues: 'Over the next generation in Britain we must re-learn how to live together successfully. The solution I advocate is not to pretend that everybody can feel the same affinity with all identities outside their own, but to build an "encounter culture" in which it becomes easier and more rewarding to interact with and respect others.'

Depressingly, Lammy notes that ties to political parties and faith groups have dwindled so much that these can no longer be relied on to provide these opportunities for encounter. His analysis, accurate or not, presents a challenge to us to remodel our churches as places where we do not go for shelter *from* the other, but go in order to *encounter* the other – whether that be our neighbour or our God. Indeed, the very idea of going *into* a building and expecting the other to come and meet us there appears to run counter to the big picture of the gospel narrative, which sees God moving *out* from the temple in order to encounter us.

So the challenge that the Church must face in being a generous place is not simply how to welcome people in, as they are doing at St Gregory of Nyssa, but also how to go out and become a community of encounter.

One example of this that a friend of mine is developing in the US is the idea of a 'big table'. By arrangement with the local authorities, a street is shut down, and down the centre of that street tables are set up. People from the local community are then simply invited to come to that table and bring and share food. This same idea has already taken off in 'The Big Lunch' – an annual national event dreamed up by Tim Smit and Paul Twivy one morning at the Eden Project, a visitor attraction in Cornwall which, through exposure to different ecologies in its huge biomes, attempts to educate people about the environment. The Big Lunch is again a very simple idea: register your willingness to host a Big Lunch party in your street, then people can see where their nearest event is and bring food to share.

Again, these examples show how encounter can be mediated through the sharing of food, and an ordinary space temporarily penetrated by something marvellous. There will be those who scoff at such events, and question whether they have the power to change anything. My answer would be that these events in themselves perhaps do not have tangible effects, but the power of the symbols that they present *will* have hidden and unknown consequences. This is the power of 'living symbolically': we know that inaction will condemn us, whether it be through laziness or cynicism. While we don't fool ourselves that our actions are going to have dramatic effects, we trust that in their symbolism there will be resonances with people that will lead to more obviously powerful changes. One would not suggest changing the way a country viewed ethnic minorities by taking a seat on a bus, but in this powerful symbolic act, Rosa Parks' simple action precipitated an historic campaign of action.

If our churches are to become 'communities of encounter' then they are going to have to be communities that are prepared to leave the security of their buildings and proactively mediate these encounters with and between others. We have already seen that the work Richard Wilkinson and Kate Pickett have done in *The Spirit Level* shows beyond doubt that greater income inequality is the most important factor in worsening almost all life outcomes in society. What is interesting is that other research has linked disadvantage to both the ability and willingness of local residents to intervene in youth violence and antisocial behaviour: those in better-off areas are more likely to intervene and do so effectively than those in poorer areas.[17] This creates a vicious circle for those growing up and living in disadvantaged areas. Not only are they more likely to experience violence, but those around them are less likely to intervene when violence breaks out. A 'socialisation divide' is thus created between the best and worst off, and it is only through agencies such as the Church, who are committed to providing encounter spaces, that this divide can be overcome.

One example of a group of people modelling this approach is the Street Pastors scheme, created by Les Isaac. Isaac sees the local church as a place where people from all parts of the community – from traders to grandmothers to fathers to shop-keepers – can gather, and because of these many connections it is therefore the natural place from which a positive influence can come to the streets at night. Groups of Street Pastors go out into the local community on weekend nights to simply be a presence. They don't go to preach, but to care, help and mediate in any way that they can. When those who have drunk too much fall out of clubs and need someone to help them get home safely, Street Pastors are on hand to help. When disagreements break out and are heading towards violent confrontation, Street Pastors – all well trained over a period of months – step in to calm matters down. Free flip-flops are given to girls whose feet are hurting, and night-bus timetables are distributed, as are warm blankets for those who have come out unprepared for a cold night. The results are impressive: in Southwark, South London, a nine-month police evaluation recorded up to a 95 per cent reduction in calls relating to public disorder whenever the Street Pastors were deployed.[18]

Schemes such as this, with Christians proactively going to the streets to engage people and help them at their point of need, should be more widespread. For many, church is a place to escape the anxiety and stress of life in the city. However, in a culture such as the one predominant in the UK's urban areas, church build-ings as places of refuge for – not from – the other, may again become important. Britain has become the most observed soci-ety on earth, with more CCTV cameras per head of population than anywhere else. With serious questions being asked about the erosion of civil liberties in this surveillance society and with so many of our encounters being mediated by screens, the ancient idea of the church as refuge – a place to escape the constant snooping, a piratical place 'beneath the map' where civil liberties are taken seriously and where people actually meet face to face – is one that should be resurrected.

These places of encounter and refuge will have an impact on the mental health of those who use them. In a chapter in *The Spirit Level* examining health and anxiety, Wilkinson and Pickett conclude from aggregating a wide range of research that: 'the most powerful sources of stress affecting health seem to fall into three intensely social categories: low social status, lack of friends, and stress in early life.'[19]

It is interesting that updated status and friendship counts are two of the key features of social networks, which are used so ubiquitously among young people to negotiate their relationships. What we must work to ensure is that the anxieties that children can feel maintaining high status on these sites does not lead to poor mental health and a poor sense of secure place as they grow up, because the data is very clear that stress and status anxiety in early life will increase the risk that they are involved in the criminal justice system.

Unfortunately, the increase in *digital* social networks has been paralleled with a decrease in *physical* social networking. With our increasingly urbanised and profit-focused society, many small local communities are being stripped of places that have traditionally mediated important low-level local encounters. Post Offices are closing, as are local shops and pubs. On the surface, the accountants will say that these businesses are not profit-making, and therefore surplus to requirements in the market economy. In the relational economy though, it is these sorts of places that actually allow communities to thrive.

In response to this, more churches should consider what they could do with their buildings to provide encounter spaces. Some churches have already allowed Post Offices to be located within them, and local shops too – simple examples of 'providing a place'. I walked through a small village recently where the local shop had relocated to the pub – making it once again truly a 'public house' where the whole community gathered, rather than just a drinking venue where the men escaped. There has been much talk in 'emerging church' circles of 'pub churches' where faith communities gather in pubs for their act of worship or discussion, but I would like to see the reverse happening too: churches being restored to their status as 'public houses' – places where the community can experience encounter. This will involve a challenge whereby we have to move from seeing our church buildings as purified sanctuaries where we can escape the problems of the world outside, to seeing them as places where dirt is given welcome – precisely what Jesus modelled when he turned over the tables of the money-changers who were denying ordinary people access to the temple. In his tirade against them, shouting 'didn't you know that this should be a house of prayer?' Jesus is effectively equating prayer with an opportunity for encounter – regardless of our state of purity.

It is in this sense of being prepared to go out and wait for the returning prodigals, *and* bringing them in to offer them a place of hospitality and welcome, that the Church needs to become 'the father'. We must reject the temptation to perform heroics – flash-in-the-pan campaigns that expend huge amounts of energy and resources but bring little long-term change – and instead be committed to the work of the parent/heir.

Becoming places of transformation: Synergy Theatre

As we develop these communities of encounter, communities that both gather in to provide refuge and go out to seek the other, there will be projects that spring from them that may well become very much 'para-church', with no obvious connection to a particular community of faith. One such example is the Synergy Theatre Company, run by a good friend, Esther Baker.

The theatre has always been a TAZ space. For a while, a stage is transformed into other places, and people take on other guises and roles in order to perform. Even in very early theatre – from Greek comedies and tragedies to rituals performed by shamans and priests – the performance has been recognised as a means of transformation. By encountering a narrative or set of actions, the audience are given funds to imagine new ways of being.

What Esther has done with Synergy is to take the transformative power of theatrical performance and locate it in and among prisoners and ex-offenders. This does two things. First, by performing plays in prisons, the audience – made up of offenders, offenders' family and friends, and others – are brought into an encounter situation in a space very different to a visitor suite. For many in the audience this will be the first time they have been into a prison or perhaps sat with those who are in prison. As Lammy has pointed out, even this low-level sort of engagement can lead to better relationships between these groups, and given that a huge amount of offending is rooted in relational dysfunction, this can only be a good thing.

Second, by fully involving offenders in the process of creating a production – whether through writing, directing, acting or stage management – Synergy are affirming what is not often admitted in professional performance: the transformative power of theatre to those performing it. Putting on a piece of high-quality theatre is hard work, and the disciplines of reading and learning lines, following direction and collaborating with others on a shared project are all excellent transferable skills that will benefit all involved.

But this is not simply a drama class. By aiming at public performance, Synergy are giving offenders a powerful sense of autonomy and self-respect as they enter their roles and play their parts. It is this sense of the possibility of playing a different role to that which society has long expected of us that makes theatre in prisons so transformative. 'What transpired is an experience over three months that will live with me forever,' says Rob, a prisoner who acted in a recent production of *Tartuffe*. Some, such as Amir, who played the lead role in Synergy's 2005 production of *On The Waterfront*, have gone on to professional acting work upon release. Others have gone into media production degrees. Others still struggle with life 'on the outside', but are at least having longer gaps between repeat offences.

Becoming places of security: the limits of TAZ

In order to discuss the place of TAZ in public life more closely I arranged a dinner conversation with Esther and two other friends, one a senior civil servant working in the UK's Cabinet Office on public policy and the other a child psychologist. I was keen to tease out whether the concept of the TAZ had anything to offer in terms of front-line work with those on the margins of our communities. Over the course of the evening we concluded that it did, but that there were real limitations when it came to effecting long-term transformation.

An example from Esther's work is instructive. An ex-offender living in London and involved heavily in Synergy's work will have the opportunity to have transformative encounters through their theatre work. But these encounters, these movements into TAZ spaces, can only be effective if they feel secure in other areas of their lives. As Esther put it, the transformative power of the Temporary Autonomous Zone can only function if the ex-offender has a Permanent Autonomous Zone in which their life can be grounded – in other words, secure accommodation, a means of supporting themselves and gaining some social standing.

It became apparent that the same was true in child psychology: TAZ as a model for engaging children in therapeutic situations is helpful, but, more importantly, they needed a secure base, a set of reliable and trustworthy relationships and a place they could call home, before this could be said to be effective.

What we might then conclude is that the TAZ model is an effective way of engaging the other – but only if the other has some kind of permanent, secure base from which they are living. For the most marginalised in society, this base has been so thoroughly eroded that TAZ engagements will be ineffective.

Again we find that the role of faith communities wishing to engage the other is two-fold. While they use TAZ as a way of bringing transformative spaces to the host community in ways that minimise any imbalance of power, they must also be reflecting on the profound need that those who are *most* marginalised will have for more permanent and secure foundations.

It is in this sense that we can re-read Jesus' words in John 14:2 that 'in my Father's house are many rooms; if it were not so, I would have told you. I am going there to prepare a place for you.' This is the essence of basic Christian hospitality that Christine Pohl is urging us towards. Being hospitable is not about shoving food in people's mouths. It is about giving them the dignity of their own room, a place that they can call their own, and arrange as they wish. These small acts of dignity may be as simple as taking over a Laundromat for an evening a week and providing coins so that the homeless and others can wash their clothes, as they do in the Laundry Love project.[20] Or they may demand larger commitments – with Christians becoming more and more involved in fostering vulnerable children, or in the parole system.

As my friend in the civil service made quite clear, this will have political implications. It may be heroic to do a mission to young offenders; it will be the work of the heir to work long term with families and impact early development of children born into poverty, to build secure play spaces and ensure that children are listened to. These are city-wide issues that will require people to involve themselves in social services, local governance and other disciplines such as applied social science and psychotherapy.

Indeed, it will have to go even deeper than that. Camila Batmanghelidjh, the Iranian-born founder of *Kids Company*, which works with some of the most severely disaffected young people in South East London, is convinced that her work can only be successful if it goes right to the roots of neurobiology.[21] The rage responses of the young people she works with are so beyond their own control that it is questionable whether they are even conscious of the wrongs they are doing when they 'lose it'. These neural patterns are created at a very young age through trauma, neglect or inadequate parenting. If we want to see genuinely transformative results it will be at these deep, long-term levels that we will have to work.

This inclusion of these other disciplines in our field of concern is hugely important if we are to practise the integrated life in God that we preach. For example, prayer ministry and laying on of hands may be good in some situations, but to focus entirely on that to the exclusion of psychotherapy is to cloister our faith into one area of life and admit that it has no place in others. It will be important for those with good theological groundings to involve themselves in these other areas like life coaching, psychotherapy, neurobiology and psychiatry in order that our encounters with the other – especially when our neighbour is marginalised and in serious need – are healing and holistic. We need to be able to offer them new cartographies and new ways of being that move beyond a life collapsed into either facticity or transcendence and back to the invigorating paradox of healthy co-existence.

Becoming peacemakers: imagining reconciliation in Israel/Palestine

I began this book at the InterContinental Hotel in Bethlehem, my thoughts under fire from drunken guests in neighbouring rooms, personal frustrations and impassioned arguments from all sides of the conflict. Healthy co-existence seemed a very long way off, the social archaeology of the land rich with conflict on every level. Religions had battled here for thousands of years, and now the divisions between Israel on the one side and fledgling Palestine on the other had calloused into a monstrous wall of concrete so immovable, so colourless and silent in its grimness, that all hope of peace was absorbed by it and disappeared.

What could Jesus' words about loving God, self and other mean in the face of such a labyrinthine conflict? Is it sensible to even hope that such large-scale international affairs can be affected by the principles we have covered here? When Jesus spoke about peace, could he really have envisaged the sorts of global problems that face us today, with inter-related geopolitical, religious, economic and even narcotic dimensions to the situations in Afghanistan, Iraq, Pakistan, Somalia and Israel/Palestine?

Perhaps he did. As the true Son of God, perhaps in blessing peacemakers as sons of God he knew something of the highest calling that bringing peace, equality and justice between one and other requires. Additionally, if we are truly to live lives committed to loving the other then we have no option but to at least hope that a manifesto of love can have an impact, even on the international stage.

John Paul Lederach – recognised worldwide for his work in reconciliation and mediation in conflicts as far afield as Nicaragua, Somalia, Northern Ireland, Tajikistan and the Phillipines – certainly thinks so, as he makes clear in his book *The Moral Imagination: The Art and Soul of Building Peace*. In this beautiful, meditative and hopeful book, Lederach argues that the capacity for us even to *imagine* peace is the first step towards peace actually breaking out: 'Time and again, where in small or large ways the shackles of violence are broken, we find a singular tap root that gives life to the moral imagination: the capacity of individuals and communities to imagine themselves in a web of relationship even with their enemies.'[22]

Violence, he notes, is simply the behaviour of someone incapable of imagining other solutions to the problem at hand. If this is the case, then central to the task of peacemaking must be funding the imagination of those enmeshed in conflict, permitting them to see that the web of relationships includes both them and their enemies. Lederach calls these times where new ways of being can be imagined 'turning points', which are 'moments pregnant with new life, which rise from what appear to be the barren grounds of destructive violence and relationships'.[23] I don't think it is stretch-ing the parallel too far to see that Lederach's 'turning points' are, by another name, the TAZ moments that I have described which, penetrated by the marvellous, 'liberate an area of land, of time, of imagination and then dissolve . . . before the State can crush them'. Lederach is certainly clear that such moments will not be manufactured by the state, nor by the technocrats that run their systems. No, 'they must be explored and understood in the context of something that approximates the artistic process, imbued as it is with creativity, skill, serendipity and craftsmanship'.

We are, in other words, back with Allan Kaplan and his thesis that those involved in social process are 'artists of the invisible'. The theologian Walter Brueggemann concurs: 'Every totalitarian regime is frightened of the artist. It is the vocation of the prophet to keep alive the ministry of imagination, to keep on conjuring and proposing futures alternative to the single one the king wants to urge as the only thinkable one.'[24]

Our work towards international peace must be, in the first place, a work of artistry rather than legislation and policy. It will be in creative spaces – holding in mind theologian Matthew Fox's definition of creativity in the title of his recent book as the place 'where the divine and human meet' – that peace will begin to built.

However, as we have seen in *The Spirit Level*, it will be economic parity that will play a large part in creating the conditions for peace too. One only need visit Israel and Palestine to be shocked by the differences in the availability of core resources such as water and green space. Huge Israeli settlements in the West Bank chan-nel vast percentages of the available water into garden sprinklers and pools, while Palestinian homes have intermittent supplies and require huge water storage tanks to make the most of the times when Israel allows their water to flow. It is made very clear that these economic disparities are actually part of Israeli policy when one visits the Arab-majority parts of Israeli-controlled Jerusalem. Here, under the same municipal governance, the pavements suddenly disappear, the rubbish collection becomes intermittent, the traffic lights do not work and the street furniture and roads are in terrible condition. Whatever the reasoning behind such policies Wilkinson and Pickett have made the outcomes of such decisions beyond question: inequality will lead to greater violence and unrest.

Work towards international peace needs to have an economic dimension as this will be part of the 'Permanent Autonomous Zone' which will lead to stability and security, and thus become a foundation for reconciliation. So if you visit Palestine, don't go in for an hour or two and get the bus straight out, but stay in a hotel in Palestine. If you buy olive oil, buy from a Fairtrade Palestinian supplier. Lobby your representatives to show your support for the European Union's Preferential Trade Agreement with Israel being made contingent on Israel improving its human rights record and abiding by international law with regard to settlement activity, freedom of movement and land appropriation.

Greater economic equality will create the conditions within which peace can prosper. But it will be artistic, TAZ moments, that foster contact at the level of individuals on the ground which Lederach sees as equally important. One example of a creative approach to this kind of contact is 'Hello Peace'. By calling a particular telephone number Israelis or Palestinians can be put through to random people within a calling circle 'on the other side'. They can shout, scream and moan at their enemies – or simply talk, and discover that those they had thought were monsters are human, fragile and desperate for peace, just as they are. To date, over a million minutes of such conversations have taken place, building a gentle groundswell of people within both populations who refuse to demonise the other, and who can now see themselves 'in a web of relationship, even with their enemies'.

Once again we see the vital importance of mediating spaces of encounter, of facilitating modes of low-level engagement so that Israelis and Palestinians can become communities who encounter one another in peaceful, non-violent and imaginative ways. David Lammy's adage that 'increasing the level of contact between different groups is enough to generate more favourable relationships between them', seems to apply internationally, as well as locally.

Two very different examples of programmes that seek to increase contact towards this goal spring to mind. Israeli-Palestinian Bereaved Families for Peace provide moments, turning points, when families from both sides who have suffered losses in the conflict can meet and talk and grieve – and overcome the pressure to caricature the enemy as a faceless, heartless other. And, at the closest, most intimate level, what better way to decrease the distance between one and the other than through a programme in which Israelis donate blood to Palestinian hospitals, and Palestinians donate their own blood for Israelis?

It is in these small acts of sustenance and recreation that the space to imagine possibilities not based on violence will emerge.[25] The conflict in Israel/Palestine has been hugely costly, not just to relationships between these two communities, but to relationships within them too. Tensions between different facets of Judaism – from Russian to American to indigenous Sephardic – continue to rumble on just below the surface of Israeli society. As Avraham Burg has so beautifully written in *The Holocaust is Over – We Must Rise from its Ashes*, complex feelings about the holocaust and its repercussions on Jews worldwide mean that the Palestinians have become a convenient common enemy, and the unimaginable tragedy of that genocide has become almost fetishised in the Israeli consciousness, actually preventing much helpful criticism of Israel's legitimate concerns about security being heard.

Similarly, the tension of living under occupation has caused huge damage to Palestinian society. Stress and depression are rife, as are family disputes and tensions between political factions and religions. Many of the (mostly more wealthy) Christians in Palestine have fled to the US or other countries. It was thus immensely moving to share dinner with local Muslims and Christians at Wi'am, a conflict resolution centre in Bethlehem. Young and old, with faith or without, we broke bread, spooned rice and meat from huge platters and drank local wine from ancient vineyards before sharing music across cultures and generations.

I have written much about the importance of food in these pages, and here was a feast in the proper TAZ sense, in the proper tradition of gift. Food is our most basic sustenance, firmly rooted in the earth under our feet. But here it was raised up to the level of spiritual nourishment, the same dishes lifted up by Muslim, Christian and Jewish hands into mouths that spoke and sang and imagined the possibility that, if only we could eat together more often, peace could break out even in this most fractured and battered of places.

It was with these complex tastes still lingering in my mouth that I left Palestine, passed through checkpoints and went through interviews and searches at airports, and lifted off from the Holy Land with a small kernel of hope still lodged in my teeth. It was, and remains a hope that that little town of Bethlehem will once again lie still under the silent stars, that in its dark streets the everlasting light will shine, and that the hopes and fears of all of us throughout history who long for peace within ourselves, among our faiths and in our communities will be met in it some night.

LIVING SYMBOLICALLY IN A MANY-BODIED WORLD

I have begun and ended in Bethlehem because this little town symbolises so many of the conflicts with the other that we face. Just outside Jerusalem, it was the place where God began to intervene. In another place just outside Jerusalem it seemed that that intervention had failed, but, just as something marvellous penetrated that young girl and brought life into being in Bethlehem, so something marvellous penetrated that cold tomb and brought life to a dead and buried body again.

Bethlehem, Golgotha. Forsaken by community, forsaken by God. These places outside Jerusalem that have experienced such horror and conflict are places where hope for something marvellous is most needed precisely because they are where the possibility of engagement with the other seems so hopeless.

What applies in Bethlehem could be equally applied to so many other conflict situations around the world. These problems seem so immense that it is tempting to forget them and simply concentrate our attention on the local, the manageable, the achievable. Yet I strongly believe that if we are to take Jesus' words about peace seriously we need to see them as applicable at all zoom levels. From the personal to the familial, communal, local, national, international and into the divine-universal our highest calling is to love the other.

Teacher, he asked, what is the greatest commandment?

You ask for a single rule of life?

Yes.

> You ask for one rule, but there can be no singularity in this
> plural world. You ask for one rule; I will say two things, about
> three loves . . .

In the face of such huge global problems like climate change, international terrorism, religious extremism, poverty, obesity, racism, mass immigration, urban blight, gang warfare, teenage alcoholism, alienation, addiction and depression, one wonders if it is ever worth acting at all. With such a list of problems ranging from the worldwide through to the national, provincial, local and personal, would it not simply be better to blinker our eyes, stupefy our minds, log on and tune out?

There will be those who claim that nothing can be done in the face of such a multi-faceted crisis: there is no society, there are only faint shadows of community left in our towns, fading traces of once-deep relationships and deeply rooted families. One might as well live for the moment, and live for oneself. I believe we must ignore those voices, though it is true that the situation we face is complex.

There is a well-known question in mathematics called the Three-Body Problem. The trajectory of one body, the future path of one particle with a given mass and initial velocity, can be calculated easily. The interaction of two bodies – a hypothetical moon orbiting a hypothetical earth – can also be calculated without much difficulty, and the paths that they will follow be predicted with some certainty. But the simple addition of a third body causes the problem to spin into total incalculability. Given just an earth, a moon and a sun, each with a mass and initial position and velocity, the future trajectory of these three interacting bodies *cannot* be calculated. There are simplifications and special cases, statistical analyses and algorithms that allow us to guess the tides and seasons with some confidence. But there can be no solution.

Love God, love your neighbour, as you love yourself. God as sun, me as ground and you as just one, orbiting other. Just the three of us form a system so complex that not even all man's mathematics, nor the machines he has built, can calculate with certainty if we will collapse into one another, spin endlessly apart or settle into some periodic stability.

Yet, even more than this, we live in a universe of near infinite bodies. The complexities of the Three-Body Problem pale into insignificance as more than six billion of us interact in this worldwide asteroid belt of varying gravities, weights and velocities. So in this sense the sceptics are right: there can be no calculation. The system *is* too complex. My movements, me, a single body in a swirling crowd of billions, are too small to matter, too crowded with complexities to compute.

To the materialist eye, this is all that can be said. But for those of us who refuse to collapse the paradox of our existence into simple material facticity, or inflate it with vain hope of total transcendence, there exists an inbetween place, a temporary, generous, heretical, artistic, loving, transforming place where the differential calculus does not reign, and where five loaves and two small fish just might equal a meal for thousands. It is a place away from the hard and calculating cartography of the empire, a place beneath the maps where the normal laws do not apply, and where a merry life of piracy and risk can be enjoyed, if only for a short while.

To dare to hope that Jesus' summary of the law into a tripartite love could make any difference at all *is* a risk. But, as John Paul Lederach points out, it is a risk that may be all we have in the face of the violence that is our daily reality: 'Risk by its very nature is mysterious. It is mystery lived, for it ventures into lands that are not controlled or charted. People living in settings of deep-rooted conflict are faced with an extraordinary irony. Violence is known; peace is the mystery. By its very nature, therefore, peacebuilding requires a journey guided by the imagination of risk.'[1]

It is to throw ourselves into this uncharted, uncontrolled and mysterious place that is the calling of those who respond to Jesus' call to love. We should not fool ourselves that we will be heroes, whose great actions will save many. Rather, we must aim to be simple heirs, working with symbols that speak of a greater reality to come.

In fact, offering symbols is sometimes all we can do in this vastly complex world. Signs point towards one thing. Symbols do not point, but rather act as conductors between two spaces, between the transcendent and the immanent, the possible and the impossible, the material and the immaterial. When Jesus lifted the bread above his head and gave thanks for it, he moved it into symbol, into a liminal space between the physicality of the bread he was touching, and the meta-physical of the bread he was becoming.

As the body of Christ in a complex world, this should continue to be our model. As the community of the now-and-not-yet, the Pirates of the Charism, we should seek to live in the risky place of mystery, in the imaginative space of symbols. This is what the role of the priest should always have been – to stand symbolically in the space between the immanent and the transcendent, and conduct.

There will be notes – crotchets and quavers of this symbolic music – for us to play at a personal level. We must embrace the clearing, the desert spaces that will allow us to grow into separate and bound selves, living in good faith. We must resist the temptation to be 'Guitar Heroes', dazzling everyone with our solo playing, and instead turn our ears to symphony, to leading others into the space where their harmonies might be heard.

There will be movements for us to appreciate at the level of the divine, isons[2] that surround and sustain all other sounds. While the essence of the piece can be codified, there will be moments of ecstatic playing that go beyond recording, beyond the strict lines of the clef. We should neither insist on a spirit-less playing that follows only the correct techniques set out in the books, nor ignore the rich history of composition and the freedom that only comes from disciplined practice.

And, all around us, there will be this rich symphony of sounds, some rising, some falling, some joyful, some lamenting – all moving the air and disturbing the *pneuma*. It is not our job to tap our batons or play God with the levels. It will simply be enough for us to trust that when we encounter one another in an attitude of love and a place of justice and equality, some deep resonance will bring forth a sweet music. This is no siren song to draw us desiring, only to smash us on the rocks. It is the polyphony of the universe, a triadic love song, the sound of a billion and more lives seeking harmony.

Teacher, of all the commandments, which is the most important?

We began our journey with a demand for a law, a simple piece of code to live all life by. As we come to our conclusion, we can be thankful that Jesus refused this simplification. We exist in multiple dimensions, and Jesus was wise enough to steer away from a list of 'do nots' to urge us towards love.

In a world of such diverse experience, one might wonder why songwriters have always returned to this subject. It is surely because love is itself a music: physical, invisible, transcendent, beautiful, healing, sorrowful, risky, immanent, generous, personal, temporary, shared, ecstatic. Very divine and very human, reliant on tools, but somehow transcending them, drawing us together, breaking down the barriers and bypassing rational understanding.

Until the seven trumpets sound, this love-song will be the closest encounter we will have with the Other. Until that great feast begins, it will be the soundtrack to all our hospitality. Until our lover returns to us, it will be the scent, the mystery, the promise and the hope of that return. And until that time, it will be the inspiration to love others as he loved us.

What kind of selves do we need to be in order to live in harmony with others?

Strangely, after all these words, it seems that the answer lies right there within. To *live* in harmony, we need only to be constantly putting ourselves in places where we can *hear* that harmony, hear that divine music that sings of love and says simply this: Dear friends, since God so loved us, we also ought to love. One and other.

Notes

Introduction

1. One soon learns travelling round this land that is called 'Holy' that there are sites that owe more to tradition than any historical accuracy, and others, like this ancient church – the oldest continually worshipping church in the world – that have very serious credentials to back up their pilgrim-site claims.
2. R. Wilkinson and K. Pickett, *The Spirit Level – Why More Equal Societies Almost Always Do Better* (Allen Lane, 2009), p. 36–7.
3. C. Pohl, *Making Room – Recovering Hospitality as a Christian Tradition* (Eerdmans, 1999), p. 4.
4. Recent research has shown that little has changed. A group of theology students were asked to prepare a sermon on the 'Good Samaritan' and were encouraged to really wrestle with it in discussion. On the route of their walk to the church where they were to preach a stooge injured man was placed on the pavement, in serious pain. When told they would be late for the service if they stopped to help, the vast majority ignored the injured man in order to be on time to preach on the 'Good Samaritan'. See the excellent 'Philosophy Bites' podcast: http://nigelwarburton.typepad.com/philosophy_bites/2009/05/walter-sinnottarmstrong-on-moral-psychology.html.
5. Pohl, *Making Room*, p. 13.
6. Lev. 19:34.
7. Pohl, *Making Room*, p. 13.
8. My own story is in the Christian tradition, and, as you will have gathered, it is mostly from this tradition that I will be drawing, but I hope that people of all faiths could find resonances in these pages. Indeed, unless they can, I will have failed in my task.

9. The play was a benefit piece for the churches of the Diocese of London, and Eliot only accepted authorship of a small part of the text.

10. Wilkinson and Pickett, *The Spirit Level*, p. 29.

Part One

1. M. Volf, *Exclusion and Embrace* (Abingdon Press, 1996), p. 21.

2. ibid.

3. S. Žižek, *Violence* (Profile, 2008), p. 7.

4. A. Kaplan, *Development Practitioners and Social Process – Artists of the Invisible* (Pluto, 2002), p. xviii.

5. ibid., p. xvii.

6. S. Žižek, *On Belief* (Routledge, 2001), pp. 13, 15.

7. Kaplan, *Development Practitioners and Social Process*, p. 64.

8. Martin Heidegger, 'The Origin of the Work of Art', 1971 (1935), p. 53.

9. S. Žižek and J. Milbank, *The Monstrosity of Christ – Paradox or Dialectic?* (MIT Press, 2009), p. 30.

10. ibid., p. 31.

11. Mark Edmundson, *Dwelling in Possibilities*, http://chronicle.com/free/v54/i27/27b00701.htm.

12. R. Sennett, *Flesh and Stone* (W.W. Norton & Company Ltd, 1994), p. 374.

13. Edmundson, *Dwelling in Possibilities*. He goes on to quote Thoreau, who drolly noted, 'We are in great haste to construct a magnetic telegraph from Maine to Texas; but Maine and Texas, it may be, have nothing important to communicate.'

14. ibid.

15. J. Margo and M. Dixon, *Freedom's Orphans – Raising Youth in a Changing World* (IPPR, 2006), p. viii.

16. R. Wilkinson and K. Pickett, *The Spirit Level – Why More Equal Societies Almost Always Do Better* (Allen Lane, 2009), p. 34.

17. Zigmunt Bauman, *Liquid Life* (Polity Press, 2005), p. 68.

18. Strangely, when writing this piece I was on a train from Edinburgh to London, sitting opposite two girls, one of whom had her arm in a

sling. They spent the entire journey talking to each other, and various characters on their mobiles, about the events of the night before. It became graphically apparent that they had got outrageously drunk, and one boy in their group had slung the girl over his shoulder, and then dropped her, breaking her collar bone. She had no memory of this. Both agreed it was a 'bloody good night. Yeah, brilliant.'

19. Those with an understanding of thermodynamics will know that under certain conditions of temperature and pressure, substances like water can reach a 'triple point' where their solid, liquid and gaseous states can exist simultaneously. The cultural parallels are obvious.

20. http://www.guardian.co.uk/uk/2009/feb/24/social-networking-site-changing-childrens-brains.

21. http://www.theatlantic.com/doc/200811/multiple-personalities/3.

22. As even the pioneer of virtual reality Jaron Lanier puts it in his brilliant thesis, *You are Not a Gadget*, which was published too recently to fully integrate into this book, 'The deep meaning of personhood is being reduced by illusions of bits.' Jaron Lanier, *You are Not a Gadget* (Allen Lane, 2010) p. 20.

23. http://networkcultures.org/wpmu/geert/2009/06/15/the-digital-given-10-web-20-theses-by-ippolita-geert-lovink-ned-rossiter/. In an interesting piece of research it was found that those with more friends were less susceptible to catching a cold virus: 'Having friends, being married, belonging to a religious group or other association and having people who will provide support, are all protective of health.' It would be interesting to see if that still held for those with more *virtual* friends too.

24. *Hedgehog Review*, vol. 5, no. 3, pp. 5–7.

25. Ivan Illich, *Tools for Conviviality* (Harper and Row, 1973), p. xii.

26. Aaron Falbel, 'The Mess We're In', in *The Challenges of Ivan Illich* (State University of New York Press, 2002), p. 131.

27. Roger Scruton, 'The Sacred and the Human', *Prospect*, August 2007.

28. Christopher Booker, *The Seven Basic Plots* (Continuum, 2004), p. 702.

29. Henri Nouwen, *The Return of the Prodigal Son* (Dartman, Longman & Todd Ltd, 1994), p. 121.

30. Michael Bywater, *Big Babies* (Granta, 2007), p. 6.

31. Nouwen, *Return of the Prodigal*, p. 121, italics mine.

32. ibid.

33. Just as in the exchange between Bagheera and Baloo in Disney's *The Jungle Book*: 'I love that boy just like my own cub,' 'Then do what's best for Mowgli, not yourself.'

34. In a recent case, a mother was found guilty of arranging the kidnap of her own daughter, with a view to claiming the reward that one or other of the tabloid newspapers were bound to offer. In the judge's verdict, her main crime was an 'inability to put your child's needs above your own'. It is this task of having to step beyond selfish childhood and into responsible parenthood, of suddenly having to think beyond the self and to the needs of another, that is proving so difficult for so many. It is too easy to point the finger at teenage criminals and binge-drinkers who have no political muscle. What is harder is for politicians to challenge parents to reflect on their own lives and do something about it.

35. Bauman, *Liquid Life*, p. 44.

36. ibid., p. 47.

37. ibid., p. 42.

38. We don't know much of Paul's impact in Rome. But not much later, it was the Roman Emperor's mother, albeit in Constantinople, who persuaded her son to adopt Christianity as the official religion of the Empire, thus changing Christianity's relationship to power forever. Of course, many thinkers have claimed, like Žižek, that 'there is no Christ outside of St Paul' and that it is futile to try to get to Christ's authentic message outside of the social institution of the church that Paul brings. But we must be careful not to elevate him above Jesus. Paul created one ossification of Jesus, but this is not the only formation possible.

39. Fowler's stages of faith can be summarised broadly as follows: Stage 1, 'intuitive-projective'; Stage 2, 'mythic-literal', where there is a strong belief in justice; Stage 3, 'synthetic-conventional', which is characterised by conformity; Stage 4, 'individuative-reflective',

which involves the struggle to take personal responsibility for beliefs; Stage 5, 'conjunctive', acknowledging paradox; Stage 6, 'universalising'– to get to this stage is rare and is often equated with enlightenment.

40. A. Stewart, *A Prophet of Grace* (Knox Press, reprinted 1980). There is no reason at all to reference this work, other than because it was written by my great-grandfather. His obituary noted that he 'preached freely in the Spirit, but was much troubled at home'. Which sums our family line up nicely.

41. We can see the parallels with the move from Fowler's Stage 3 into the doubt and darkness of Stage 4.

42. D. Paterson, *The Book of Shadows* (Picador, 2004), p. 39.

43. S. Žižek, *On Belief*, p. 146.

44. S. Žižek, *Violence*, p. 133.

45. See http://www.kesterbrewin.com/tag/neophilia-and-fantasy-church/ for my blog series on this.

46. Christopher Booker, *The Neophiliacs* (Pimlico, 1992), p. 352 (originally published by Collins in 1969, nicely predating and anticipating punk, the music that was the final 'deathwish' of the rock-and-roll of the 60s).

47. ibid.

48. *The Believer*, Feb. 2009, p. 61.

49. C. Plantinga, *Not The Way It's Supposed To Be: A Breviary of Sin* (Freedman, 1995), p. 29. Quoted in Volf, *Exclusion and Embrace*, p. 65.

50. ibid., p. 67.

51. ibid.

52. W. Brueggemann, *The Prophetic Imagination* (Fortress Press, 1978), p. 17.

Part Two

1. J. Milbank, *The Ethics of Self Sacrifice*, http://www.firstthings.com/article.php3?id_article=3119, March 1999.

2. With thanks to Peter Leithart in *Derrida and Gift*, http://www.leithart.com/archives/002003.php.

3. Milbank, *Ethics of Self Sacrifice*.

4. ibid.

5. As Albert Einstein quipped, 'the environment is everything that isn't me'.

6. Having looked around the floor of my 'emerging church' conferences, I think many delegates would have voted broadband, or wireless access points at least, as better than God, period.

7. Prayer, though, may actually be quite like Real Snail Mail, a system devised by Bournemouth University whereby emails are sent to an RFID chip glued to the shell of an actual snail, and only passed on to the recipient when that snail happens to pass by a receiver in a different part of the tank. Messages might therefore take days, or weeks, to arrive. See http://news.bbc.co.uk/1/hi/technology/7458531.stm.

8. See M. Kumar, *Quantum: Einstein, Bohr and the Great Debate About the Nature of Reality* (Icon, 2008).

9. http://en.wikipedia.org/wiki/Uncertainty_Principle.

10. However, most physicists still hold to the hope that a new theory will be developed which will fit with the philosophical worldview of an independent reality. As Kumar pointed out in correspondence on this, it's always unwise to build a philosophy on top of a scientific theory.

11. J. Piper, *Brothers We Are Not Professionals* (Broadman and Holman, 2002), p. 2.

12. J. Diamond, *Guns, Germs and Steel* (Chatto & Windus, 1997), p. 73.

13. According to Plutarch, Aristotle advised Alexander the Great to treat non-Greeks 'as though they were plants or animals'. See *Atlantic Magazine*, April 2009, p. 53.

14. The final irony of Pizarro's slaughter of the Incas is that it was the Incas' lack of immunity from the livestock-borne diseases that killed far more than Spanish guns ever did. They caught 'common colds' and simply died en masse.

15. See http://freegan.org.uk.

16. W. Brueggemann, *The Prophetic Imagination* (Fortress Press, 1978), p. 17.

17. R. Wilkinson and K. Pickett, *The Spirit Level – Why More Equal Societies Almost Always Do Better* (Allen Lane, 2009), p. 133.

18. S. Žižek and J. Milbank, *The Monstrosity of Christ – Paradox or Dialectic?* (MIT Press, 2009), p. 38.

19. G. Simmel, quoted in R. Sennett, *The Craftsman* (Penguin, 2008), p. 13.

Part Three

1. A. A. Milne, 'King John's Christmas', from *Now We Are Six*. Text copyright © The Trustees of the Pooh Properties 1928. Published by Egmont UK Ltd London and used with permission.

2. Henri Nouwen, *The Return of the Prodigal Son* (Dartman, Longman & Todd Ltd, 1994), p. 41.

3. ibid., p. 42.

4. A. Kaplan, *Development Practitioners and Social Process – Artists of the Invisible* (Pluto, 2002), p. xviii.

5. Luke 7:36–50.

6. *The Internet Encyclopaedia of Philosophy*, http://www.iep.utm.edu/d/derrida.htm#H7.

7. ibid.

8. P. Rollins, *How (Not) To Speak of God* (Paraclete Press, 2006), p. 70.

9. C. Levi-Strauss, *The Raw and the Cooked* (1964; University of Chicago Press, 1983), p. 18.

10. J. Milbank, *The Ethics of Self Sacrifice*, http://www.firstthings.com/article.php3?id_article=3119, March 1999.

11. Henri Nouwen, *Return of the Prodigal*, p. 121. I am painfully aware of the difficulties that this choice of metaphor may bring, especially to those who have struggled to conceive or are not in a position to do so. Having thought carefully about it, I choose to persist with the metaphor of parent because, good or bad, it is an experience that all of us can relate to. It is, however, a metaphor only.

12. M. Sandel, 'The Case Against Perfection', *Atlantic Magazine*, April 2004.

13. The writer Ezra Pound once suggested that money should be made of vegetables, so that it couldn't be pooled and hoarded or it would rot. Perhaps he was on to something.

14. R. Kapuscinski, *The Other* (Verso, 2008), p. 21.

15. A. Dworkin, 'The Case for Minor Utopias', *Prospect Magazine*, July 2007, p. 43.

16. In true anarchist style, the full text of it is available online for free at http://www.hermetic.com/bey/taz3.html#labelTAZ.

17. Bey (also known as Peter Lamborn Wilson) is a controversial figure, even in anarchist circles, who studied at Columbia University before travelling extensively in the Middle East and Asia. In 1974 he became director of English-language publications at the Imperial Iranian Academy of Philosophy in Tehran, and mysticism, Sufism and neopaganism have been themes in his work ever since. I'm well aware of the controversial nature of some of Bey's work, but it can only be a correct Christian position to believe that the least of us can say some good stuff once in a while. I certainly hope so.

18. H. Bey, *T.A.Z.* (Autonomedia, 2003), p. 95.

19. ibid., p. 101.

20. ibid., p. 99.

21. J. Derrida, *The Gift of Death* (Chicago University Press, 1996), p. 68.

22. http://www.firstthings.com/article.php3?id_article=3119.

23. See http://en.wikipedia.org/wiki/Sicarii.

24. Kapuscinski, *Other*, p. 61.

25. ibid. p. 34. Kapuscinski goes on to berate Marshall McLuhan for his term 'the global village' which he says, 'has proved to be one of the greatest mistakes of modern culture, because the essence of a village depends on the fact that its inhabitants know each other well, commune with each other and share a common fate. Meanwhile nothing of the kind can be said of society on our planet, which is more like the anonymous crowd at a major airport, a crowd of people rushing along in haste, mutually indifferent and ignorant.'

26. http://www.hermetic.com/bey/tourism.html.

27. Kapuscinski, *Other*, p. 83.

28. Amos 5:23–4.

29. Kapuscinski, *Other*, p. 35.

30. P. Lamborn Wilson, *Pirate Utopias* (Autonomedia, 1995), p. 22.

31. Nor would I want to excuse the rise of piracy we have recently seen in countries like Somalia. However, rather than simply dismiss these modern pirates as immoral thieves, we would be wise to consider, just as in the case of the seventeenth-century situation, *why* these people have turned to this way of life. A look at the local complexity of the situation reveals that many of those who have turned to piracy were fishermen. They can't fish any more because European trawlers have completely exhausted fish stocks in the region, and the seas have been polluted by foreign vessels dumping toxic waste off the Somali coast, knowing that the total lack of government would mean they could do it with impunity. (I am grateful to Alistair Ferni, head of DFID's office for Kenya and Somalia for pointing this out in conversation in Nairobi in April 2009.) As Thomas Pakenham makes it very clear in his comprehensive work *The Scramble for Africa* (Abacus, 1992), from 1876 to 1912 the entire continent was carved up among European nations. Why? The excuse was to eradicate the Arab slave trade from East Africa, but the reason was because 'the interior is mostly a magnificent and healthy country of unspeakable riches'. So perhaps Somalis feel just a little justified in dabbling in a little stealing and extortion too. An engaging article in the April 2009 edition of *Vanity Fair* describes the hostage taking of a luxury French vessel – noting that the ship was registered in a far-flung and long forgotten French protectorate in order to bypass European taxes and employment law. Although fed well, the crew were paid poorly and had appalling terms of employment.

32. ibid., p. 200.

33. L. Hyde, *Trickster Makes This World: Mischief, Myth and Art* (North Point Press, 1999), p. 177.

34. Lamborn Wilson, *Pirate Utopias*, p. 194.

35. M. Volf, *Exclusion and Embrace* (Abingdon Press, 1996), p. 21.

36. Kapuscinski, *Other*, p. 35.

37. ibid., p. 34.
38. S. Žižek and J. Milbank, *The Monstrosity of Christ – Paradox or Dialectic?* (MIT Press, 2009), p. 38.
39. ibid., p. 81.
40. See http://allafrica.com/stories/200709040132.html.
41. See http://www.christianitytoday.com/ct/2006/marchweb-only/113-23.0.html.

Part Four

1. J. Eckhart, translated O. Davies, 'On Detachment and Possessing God', in *Selected Writings* (Penguin, 1994), p. 11.
2. J. Cascio, 'Get Smarter', *Atlantic Magazine*, July/August 2009.
3. Remarks made on BBC's *Question Time*, 11 March 2009.
4. See http://www.timesonline.co.uk/tol/comment/faith/article6513866.ece.
5. G. Nicholson, in *The Believer*, June 2009, p. 68.
6. L. Freeman, *The Inner Pilgrimage: The Journey of Meditation* (Mediomedia, 2007), p. 51. This is Father Laurence Freeman's short book exploring the background and benefits of Christian meditation. The quoted passage is printed under the heading 'How to Meditate' at the back of the book.
7. T. Merton, *Thoughts in Solitude* (Burns & Oaks, 1975), p. 48.
8. O. James, *Affluenza* (Vermilion, 2007), p. 223.
9. S. Žižek and J. Milbank, *The Monstrosity of Christ – Paradox or Dialectic?* (MIT Press, 2009), p. 37.
10. H. Bey, *T.A.Z.* (Autonomedia, 2003), p. 99.
11. ibid., p. 109.
12. One metaphor Ikon have used to describe this is of a barman running a bar. The barman's responsibility is not to go round ensuring that everyone is getting on well together in the bar; his responsibility is to create a space within which this sort of care and wellbeing is fostered.
13. K. Barth, *Church Dogmatics* 1:2, 'The Doctrine of the Word of God'.
14. See http://www.guardian.co.uk/lifeandstyle/2009/jul/12/chronic-fatigue-stress-modern-life.

15. See the interview with Sara Miles at http://www.pbs.org/wnet/religionandethics/week1039/profile.html#.

16. See http://www.prospectmagazine.co.uk/2006/04/closeencounters/.

17. See the IPPR report on 'Freedom's Orphans' available at http://www.ippr.org/publicationsandreports/publication.asp?id=496.

18. http://www.timesonline.co.uk/tol/life_and_style/article548263.ece.

19. R. Wilkinson and K. Pickett, *The Spirit Level – Why More Equal Societies Almost Always Do Better* (Allen Lane, 2009), p. 39.

20. See 'The Laundry Love' project at http://just4one.org/laundrylove.html.

21. See http://news.bbc.co.uk/1/hi/uk/7588711.stm.

22. J. P. Lederach, *The Moral Imagination: The Art and Soul of Building Peace* (Oxford University Press, 2005), p. 34.

23. ibid., p. 29.

24. W. Brueggemann, *The Prophetic Imagination* (Fortress Press, 2001), p. 40.

25. It is worth noting that Lederach is a huge fan of the theory of emergence and complexity as it applies to peacemaking. See *Moral Imagination*, pp 31–4.

Conclusion

1. J. P. Lederach, *The Moral Imagination: The Art and Soul of Building Peace* (Oxford University Press, 2005), p. 39.

2. An ison is a bass note in Byzantine music; a note that is the foundation of harmony and melody.